REGULATIONS

FOR THE

DRESS

OF

GENERAL, STAFF, AND REGIMENTAL OFFICERS

OF

THE ARMY.

ADJUTANT-GENERAL'S OFFICE, HORSE GUARDS,
1857.

The Naval & Military Press Ltd

published in association with

ROYAL ARMOURIES

ROYAL
ARMOURIES

The Library & Archives Department at the Royal Armouries Museum, Leeds, specialises in the history and development of armour and weapons from earliest times to the present day. Material relating to the development of artillery and modern fortifications is held at the Royal Armouries Museum, Fort Nelson.

For further information contact:
Royal Armouries Museum, Library, Armouries Drive,
Leeds, West Yorkshire LS10 1LT
Royal Armouries, Library, Fort Nelson, Down End Road, Fareham PO17 6AN

Or visit the Museum s website at
www.armouries.org.uk

In reprinting in facsimile from the original, any imperfections are inevitably reproduced and the quality may fall short of modern type and cartographic standards.

GENERAL ORDER.

HORSE GUARDS,
1st *April* 1857.

THE QUEEN having been pleased to approve of the Dress of the Officers of the Army being established according to the following descriptions, His Royal Highness The General Commanding in Chief has received Her Majesty's commands to enjoin the strictest attention thereto; and His Royal Highness accordingly holds all General Officers, Colonels of Regiments, and Commanding Officers of Corps, responsible that these Orders for regulating the Dress shall be scrupulously obeyed.

The General Commanding in Chief has received Her Majesty's special commands to declare, that any Colonel or Commanding Officer who shall take upon himself to introduce or sanction the addition of any ornament, lace, or embroidery, or to sanction a deviation from the approved patterns in any respect whatsoever, without due authority being previously obtained for that purpose, will incur Her Majesty's displeasure.

By Command of
GENERAL
HIS ROYAL HIGHNESS
THE DUKE OF CAMBRIDGE,
K.G., G.C.B., K.P., G.C.M.G.

Commanding-in-Chief,

G. A. WETHERALL
Adjutant General.

CONTENTS.

General Officers.

Dress of Field Marshal	12
Horse Furniture for ditto	15
Dress of General	16
———Lieutenant-General	18
———Major-General	18
———Brigadier-General	19
Horse Furniture for General Officers	19
Dress of Colonel on the Staff	20

Staff Officers.

Dress of Adjutant-General ———Quarter-Master General	{ when holding the rank of General Officers }	23
———Deputy Adjutant-General ———Dep.-Qr.-Master-General	Do.	25
———Adjutant-General ———Qr.-Master-General	{ Under the rank of General Officers }	25
———Deputy-Adjutant-General ———Dep.-Qr.-Master-General	Do.	28
———Assistant Adjutant-General ———Assistant Quarter-Master General		28
———Dep.-Assistant-Adjutant-General ———Dep.-Assistant-Qr.-Master-General	{ If Field Officers }	29
———Dep.-Assistant-Adjutant-General ———Dep.-Assistant-Qr.-Master-General	{ If not Field Officers }	29
———Major of Brigade		30
Horse Furniture for Staff Officers		30

Personal Staff attached to General Officers.

Dress of Military Secretary to the Commander-in-Chief - - 32
———— Military Secretaries and Assistant Military Secretaries, if holding the rank of Field Officer - - } 32
———— Ditto (under the rank of Field Officer) - - 33
———— Aides-de-Camp to the Queen - - - 33
Horse Furniture for ditto - - - - - 36
Dress of Aides-de-Camp to General Officers - - 37
Horse Furniture for Officers composing the Personal Staff of General Officers - - - - - } 39

Dress of Staff of Recruiting Districts - - -
———————— Inspectors of Militia - - - } 40
———————— Adjutant of Recruiting Districts and Sub-Inspectors of Militia - - - 40
———————— Paymasters of Recruiting Districts - - 41

Staff of Garrisons.

Dress of Governor - - - - - - 42
———— Lieutenant-Governor - - - - 43
———— Fort or Town Major - - - - 43
———— Fort or Town Adjutant - - - - 45

Royal Military College.

Dress of Governor - - - - -
———— Lieutenant-Governor - - - -
———— Captains of Companies - - - -
———— Adjutant - - - - - } 46
———— Quarter-Master - - - -
———— Riding-Master - - - -
———— Medical Officers - - - -

Royal Military Asylum.

Dress of Commandant and other Officers	47

Cavalry Depôt.

Dress of Commandant and other Officers	48

Garrison of Chatham.

Dress of Commandant	49
—— Staff-Captain	49
—— Paymaster and Adjutant	49
Horse Furniture	49
Dress of Officers of Provisional and Depôt Battalions	50
—— Staff Officers employed in the Pay and Organization of Out-Pensioners	50
—— Officers of Medical Staff Corps	52
Dress of Provost Marshal	53

Civil Departments.

Dress of Medical Department	54
—— Commissariat Department	57
—— Judge Advocate	60
Dress of General Officers of Hussars	62

Officers of Regiments of Cavalry.

Dress of Life Guards	68
—— Royal Regiment of Horse Guards	76
—— Dragoon Guards and Heavy Dragoons	80
—— Light Dragoons	85
—— Hussars	89
—— Lancers	93
Horse Furniture for Officers of all Cavalry Regiments, the Household Brigade excepted.	97
Military Train	103

Officers of Regiments of Infantry.

Dress of Foot Guards	110
——— Infantry of the Line	116
——— Light Infantry	121
——— Fusiliers	122
——— Highland Regiments	123
——— Rifle Regiments	126
Horse Furniture for mounted Officers of Infantry	129
Dress of Cape Mounted Rifles	130
——— West India Regiments	132
——— Royal Newfoundland Companies	132
——— Royal Malta Fencibles	132
——— School of Musketry	132
——— Gold Coast Corps Artillery	133
Dress of Unattached Officers, and Officers on Half-Pay	134
——— Officers who have retired on Full-Pay	135
——— Officers who have left the Army, but whose names are allowed to remain in the Army List	135
Dress of Royal Artillery	136
——— Royal Engineers	144
——— Officers of Field Train Department	150
——— Barrack Masters	151
——— Civil Department of the Ordnance	152
Dress of Equerries to the Queen	154
——— Equerries to the Royal Family	154

GENERAL

AND

STAFF OFFICERS.

NOTE.—An Appendix will be hereafter published, containing coloured illustrations drawn in scale of the Dress and Equipments of every grade of Officer and of every Regiment in Her Majesty's Service.

The description in letter-press and in drawings in scale of the whole Equipments of Non-commissioned Officers and Rank and File, of Cavalry and Infantry, will appear in the Appendix.

GENERAL AND STAFF OFFICERS.

The *Dress* Uniform is to be worn at Levees and Drawing-rooms, and on all occasions on which the Troops are in full uniform, except upon the line of march, when the Frock-Coat is to be worn.

The blue Frock-Coat may be worn by General and Staff Officers on common occasions off Parade, and on occasions when the Troops appear in Shell-Jackets, and upon the March.

Officers of other ranks on the Staff may wear, on the occasions specified in the last paragraph, the blue Frock-Coat prescribed for them.

Staff Officers who attend in Uniform as Spectators of a Review or Inspection, are to appear in the Uniform of their respective Departments,—*not* in the blue Frock-Coat.

When the Waist-Belt is worn over the Coat, and the Sword is hooked up, the edge must be turned to the rear, and the back of the Sword to the front.

The Sash is to be worn diagonally over the left shoulder, and the end of the fringe not to hang below the bottom of the Coat.

The Dress and Horse Equipments of a General Officer of Hussars are given at page 62. The special sanction of Her Majesty must be granted for the adoption of this Uniform by General Officers. Permissions to this effect once accorded, the Dress is always to be worn, except where the Officer may be a Colonel of a Regiment of another branch of the Service, when he may also wear the uniform of his Regiment.

The Rank and Department of Officers on the General Staff of the Army are distinguished by the lace and badges on their

Cuffs and Collars, patterns of which are deposited at the Army Clothing Department.

The size and form of the buttons for all Generals, and Staff and Regimental Officers of Infantry, and Heavy Cavalry, are to correspond with the Infantry sealed pattern deposited at the Army Clothing Department. Patterns of buttons, lace embroidery, collars, badges and Regimental devices, and of Badges for Horse Furniture of Staff Officers (under the rank of General Officers), and of Regimental Field Officers, and of the Horse Equipments for all Cavalry Officers, except the Household Brigade, are deposited at the Army Clothing Department. Sealed patterns of distinctive badges, lace, Forage Cap badges, will be sent to every Regiment in the Service, and Commanding Officers are held responsible that no departure therefrom be permitted.

On all occasions on which the Queen is present, Officers in Uniform are to appear in Full Dress. The Riband of any Order of Knighthood is to be worn on those occasions over the Coat.

Officers in mourning, when dressed in uniform, are to wear a piece of black crape round the left arm, above the elbow.

FIELD MARSHAL.

Coat—Tunic, scarlet, single breasted, with fly inch and three quarters broad on the inside, with eight buttons at equal distances, with blue collar and cuffs. The collar rounded off in front, and laced round the top and bottom with inch lace. At each end of the collar, two crossed batons, formed of crimson velvet and gold, upon a wreath of laurel embroidered in silver. The cuff $10\frac{1}{2}$ inches round, three inches and a quarter deep, with two rows of inch lace round the top, leaving a light between; scarlet pointed slashed flap* on the sleeve, five inches and a half high, and two inches broad, with three buttons, and laced with inch lace. On the left shoulder a double gold cord, to retain the sash, with a small button. Two buttons at the hip. Scarlet flap on the skirt behind, ten inches deep, two inches wide, with three buttons, exclusive of those on the hip, and laced with inch lace. The edges of the back skirts laced with half-inch lace. The skirt $10\frac{1}{2}$ inches deep for an Officer five feet nine inches in height, with a variation of half an inch longer or shorter for every inch of difference in the height of the wearer. The coat, collar, cuffs, and flaps, edged with white cloth, quarter-inch broad, and the skirts lined with white.

Lace—gold, oak-leaf pattern.

Buttons—gilt, of the size and form approved by Her Majesty for the Infantry, sealed pattern of which is deposited at the Army Clothing Department, with two batons crossed, encircled with laurel.

Hat—cocked, without binding; the fan, or back part, nine inches; the front, seven and a half inches; each corner five inches; black ribbons on the two front sides.

Double Bullion Loop—gold, seven and a half inches long, with Field Marshal's button, and black silk cockade.

Tassels—flat gold worked head, six gold bullions an inch and three quarters deep, with five crimson silk bullions under them.

Plume—of white swan feathers, drooping outwards, eight inches long from the top of the wire, with scarlet feathers underneath, of sufficient length to reach the ends of the white ones; feathered stems three and a half inches in length.

Stock—black silk.

---

* NOTE.—All slashes, for every rank, whether on cuffs or skirts, are to be pointed.

Pantaloons—white leather.
Boots—jacked.
Spurs—gilt, with straps and buckles.

Or,

Trousers—blue cloth, with gold oak-leaf lace, two inches and a half wide, down the outward seam.
Boots—Wellington.
Spurs—screw, yellow metal, crane neck two inches long.

Sword—Mameluke gilt hilt, with device of two batons crossed, and encircled with oak-leaves; ivory gripe scymitar blade.

Scabbard—brass.

Sword-Knot—crimson and gold cord, with acorn end.

Sword-Belt—gold oak-leaf lace, an inch and a half wide; sword carriages of the same, one inch wide; crimson morocco lining and edging; a gilt hook to hook up the sword. The belt to be worn over the coat.

Plate—a round clasp gilt, having on the centre-piece a crown, the crossed batons, and a wreath of oak and laurel leaves, all in silver; on the outer circle a laurel wreath in dead and bright gold.

Sash—gold and crimson silk net, the ends united by a runner of platted gold and crimson; flat tassels of loose gold bullion fringe. Worn over the left shoulder, and the ends of the fringe not to hang below the bottom of the coat.

Gloves—white leather.

Frock-Coat—blue, double breasted; blue velvet collar and cuffs, the collar rounded off in front, with the crossed batons on the collar. The cuff $10\frac{1}{2}$ inches round and three inches and a quarter deep. Two rows of buttons down the front, eight in each row at equal distances, the space between the rows eight inches at top, and four at bottom; flaps on skirts behind, eleven inches deep, two inches wide, and with three buttons. The skirts seventeen inches deep for an Officer five feet nine inches in height, with a variation of half an inch longer or shorter for each inch of difference in the height of the wearer; the skirts lined with black; a double gold cord with a small button on left shoulder to retain the sash.

Undress Trousers—Oxford mixture cloth, with a scarlet stripe down the outward seam, two inches and a half wide, and welted at the edges; to be worn with the blue frock-coat.

Forage-Cap—blue cloth with gold embroidered peak, and band of gold oak-leaf lace, two inches wide, round the cap.

Great-Coat—dark blue milled cloth, double breasted; six regulation buttons; lappels $5\frac{1}{2}$ inches at top, $3\frac{3}{4}$ at bottom, lined with scarlet rattinett; blue round cuffs six inches deep; stand up collar $4\frac{1}{2}$ inches wide, blue cloth outside and lined with blue velvet; opening behind 19 inches, with four regulation buttons. Pockets in front and one inside left breast, opened at sides with pointed flaps and three buttons. Waist-belt across back to button on. Blue cape to button on, 26 inches deep and lined with red; four small regulation buttons in front and two hooks in collar.

HORSE FURNITURE.

Saddle-Cloth—blue cloth, three feet two inches in length, two feet two inches in depth, trimmed with two rows of gold oak-leaf inch and a half lace, showing a light between. The hind corners ornamented with an embroidered badge of two crossed batons, formed of crimson velvet and gold, upon a laurel wreath in silver.

The Holsters—to have fronts of blue cloth rounded to a point, with the same trimming and badge, and cloth flounces, corresponding in form, trimmed with the double lace only; pipes with gilt caps chased; double row of pointed leaves.

Bridle—of black leather, with chased gilt whole buckles; branch bit, with pad; cheeks of the shell pattern; open tails, with bolts and rings, and gilt water chain; gilt bosses with

V.R. in centre, and two batons crossed underneath encircled with laurel and crown at top.

Bridoon, Head-Stall, and Rein—of one inch gold lace lined with red morocco; blue front and roses.

Breastplate and Crupper—with gilt ornaments and buckles.

Stirrups—gilt, square set, oval bottoms, sides engraved with oak leaf. Top to cover the eye, and to bear baton and crown in relief.

Girths—blue.

Saddle—plain, gilt metal cantle.

GENERAL.

Coat—Tunic, scarlet, single breasted, with fly inch and three quarters broad on the inside, thus buttoning well over, with blue collar and cuffs, the collar rounded off in front, and laced round the top and bottom with inch lace; a silver embroidered crown and star, inch and a quarter, at each end of the collar. The cuff round, three inches and a quarter deep, ten and a half inches wide, with two rows of inch lace at the top, leaving a light between; scarlet **slashed flap to the sleeve, five inches and a half high and two inches broad,** with three buttons, and laced with inch lace. On the left shoulder a double gold cord to retain the sash, with a button. Eight buttons down the front, at equal distances. Two buttons at the waist. Scarlet flap on the skirt, ten inches deep, two inches wide, with three buttons, and laced with inch lace. The edges of the **back skirts laced with half-inch lace. The skirt 10½ inches deep for an Officer five feet nine inches in height, with a variation of half an inch longer or shorter for every inch of difference in the height of the wearer.** The coat, collar, cuffs, and flaps edged with white, a quarter of an inch in breadth, and the skirts lined with white. Buttons **of uniform size except that on the shoulder, which is to be small.**

Lace—gold, oak-leaf pattern.

Buttons—gilt, of size and form prescribed for the Infantry, with sword and baton crossed, encircled with laurel.

Hat—cocked, without binding; the fan, or back part, nine inches; the front seven and a half inches; each corner five inches; black ribbons on the two front sides.

Double Bullion Loop—gold, seven and a half inches long, with regulation button and black silk cockade.

Tassels—flat gold worked head; six gold bullions one inch and three quarters deep, with five crimson silk bullions under them.

Plume—of white swan feathers, drooping outwards, eight inches long from the top of the wire, with scarlet feathers underneath, of sufficient length to reach the ends of the white ones; feathered stem three and a half inches in length.

Stock—black silk.

Trousers—blue cloth, with gold oak-leaf lace, two inches and a half wide, down the outward seam.

Boots—Wellington.

Spurs—screw, yellow metal, crane neck two inches long.

Sword—Mameluke gilt hilt, with the device of sword and baton crossed, and encircled with oak leaves; ivory gripe; scymitar blade.

Scabbard—brass.

Sword-Knot—crimson and gold cord, with acorn end.

Sword-Belt—gold oak-leaf lace, one inch and a quarter wide, with sword carriages of the same, one inch wide; crimson morocco lining and edging; a gilt hook to hook up the sword. The belt to be worn over the coat.

Plate—a round clasp with V. R. and the crown on the centre piece, and a wreath of laurel on the outer circle; all gilt.

Sash—gold and crimson silk net, the ends united by a runner of platted gold and crimson; flat tassels of gold fringe, eight inches and a half long. Worn diagonally over the left shoulder, and the ends of the fringe not to hang below the bottom of the coat.

Gloves—white leather.

Frock-Coat—blue, double-breasted, with two rows of regulation buttons, eight in each row at equal distances. The rows two inches and a quarter apart at bottom, and three and a quarter at top. Blue velvet stand-up collar, rounded off in front, with a crown and star embroidered in gold at each end. Blue velvet round cuff, two inches and a half deep. On the left shoulder a small gold cord, with a small button, to retain the sash, which is to be worn over the shoulder.

Trousers, Undress—Oxford mixture cloth, with a scarlet stripe down the outward seam, two inches and a half wide, and welted at the edges, strapped with black patent leather like cavalry; to be worn with the blue frock-coat only.

Forage-Cap—blue cloth, with gold embroidered peak, and band of gold oak-leaf lace, two inches wide, round the cap, according to the pattern deposited at Army Clothing Department.

Great-Coat—same as laid down for F. M., but with the buttons of the rank. Page 15.

LIEUTENANT-GENERAL.

The uniform and appointments of a Lieutenant-General are the same as those of a General, with the exception that on the collar of the scarlet coat, and of the blue frock, there is only a crown at each end.

MAJOR-GENERAL.

The same as above, excepting the collar of the scarlet coat, and of the blue frock, which have a star only at each end.

BRIGADIER-GENERAL.

The uniform and appointments of a Brigadier-General are the same as those of a General Officer, except in the following particulars:—

The scarlet coat, instead of the oak-leaf lace above described, is laced throughout with gold half-inch lace of the staff pattern, and has the crown and star embroidered in silver at each end of the collar.

The blue frock coat has a plain velvet collar, without badge.

The trousers have a lace of the staff pattern, two inches and a half wide, down the outer seam.

The forage-cap has a band of lace, of the same pattern, an inch and three-quarters wide.

HORSE FURNITURE
FOR
GENERAL OFFICERS.

Saddle—hunting.

Saddle-Cloth—blue cloth, three feet two inches in length, two feet two inches in depth, trimmed with two rows of gold oak-leaf inch-and-half lace, showing a light between; and to bear the undermentioned ornaments embroidered in silver at the hind corners, according to the rank of the Officer, viz.:

The Saddle-Cloth—of a *General*, to be denoted by a crown and star.

————————— of a *Lieutenant-General*, by a crown.

————————— of a *Major-General*, by a star.

————————— of a *Brigadier-General*, by the two rows of lace only.

The Holsters—to have petticoat bags of blue cloth, rounded to a point, with the same trimming, and the badge of the

Officer's rank, and cloth flounces corresponding in form, trimmed with the double lace only. With undress the holsters to be covered with black bearskin, except in tropical climates, when they are to be covered with black leather.

Bridle—black leather, with chased gilt whole buckles; branch bit, with pads; cheeks of the shell pattern; open tails, with bolts and rings, and steel water chain; gilt bosses, with V.R. in centre, sword and baton underneath, encircled with laurel and crown at top.

Bridoon—blue front and roses.

Breastplate and Crupper—with gilt bosses and buckles.

COLONEL ON THE STAFF.

Coat—Tunic, scarlet, single-breasted, with fly on inside inch and three-quarters broad, with blue collar and cuffs. The collar rounded off in front, and laced round the top and bottom with half-inch lace; a crown and star embroidered in silver at each end of the collar. The cuff, ten and a half inches round and two inches and three-quarters deep, with two rows of half-inch lace round the top, showing a light between. Scarlet-slashed flap on the sleeve, six inches long and two inches and a quarter wide, laced at the edge, with three large buttons, and loops of half-inch lace. On the left shoulder a crimson silk cord to retain the sash, with a large button. Eight buttons down the front, at equal distances. The skirt $10\frac{1}{2}$ inches deep for an Officer five feet nine inches in height, with a variation of half an inch longer or shorter for each inch of difference in the height of the wearer. Scarlet flaps on the skirts behind, ten inches deep, and laced at the edge; two buttons on flap and one on waist, with three loops of lace. The edges of the back skirts laced with half-inch lace. The coat, collar, cuffs, and flaps edged with white cloth a quarter of an inch, and the skirts lined with white.

Lace—gold, staff, half-inch width.

Buttons—gilt, convex, of form and size prescribed for infantry, frosted, the edge encircled with burnished laurel.

Hat—cocked, without binding; the fan, or back part, nine inches and a half; the front seven and a half inches, each corner five inches; black ribbons on the two front sides.

Loop—of three-quarter inch gold lace, with regulation button, and black silk cockade.

Tassels—flat netted purl head; gold crape fringe, an inch and five-eighths deep, with crimson crape fringe underneath.

Plume—of red and white upright swan feathers, five and a half inches long from the stem to the ends of the feathers, and the whalebone quite stiff.

Stock—black silk.

Trousers—blue cloth with a stripe of gold lace, staff pattern, one and three-quarter inches wide, down the outward seam.

Boots—Wellington.

Spurs—screw, yellow metal, crane neck two inches long.

Sword—gilt three-quarter basket hilt, with device of sword and baton crossed; straight sabre blade, with rounded back, thirty-four inches long.

Scabbard—brass.

Sword-Knot—gold and crimson lace strap, with acorn end.

Sword-Belt—Russia leather, with two stripes of gold embroidery; carriages embroidered on one side only; to be worn over the coat.

Plate—gilt, having the letters V.R. with the crown above, the motto "Dieu et mon droit" below, and an oak-branch on each side, all in silver.

Sash—crimson silk net with fringe ends, united by a crimson runner. Worn diagonally over the left shoulder. The ends of the fringe not to hang lower than the bottom of the coat.

Gloves—white leather.

Frock-Coat—blue, double-breasted, with stand-up cloth collar, cloth cuffs, and regulation buttons. The collar rounded off in front, with a crown and star embroidered in gold at each end of it. Round cuff, two inches and three-quarters deep, slashed flap on sleeve five inches and a quarter long, one inch and a half wide, with three small buttons. Two rows of buttons down the front, nine in each row, at equal distances, the distance between the rows eight inches at top, four at bottom. Flaps on skirts behind, ten inches deep, with two buttons on flap and one on waist. The skirt seventeen inches deep for an Officer five feet nine inches in height, with a variation of half an inch longer or shorter for each inch of difference in the height of the wearer. The skirts lined with black. On the left shoulder a crimson silk cord, with a small button to retain the sash, which is to be worn over the shoulder.

Undress Trousers—Oxford mixture—as for Staff Officers under the rank of Major-General, to be worn only with the blue frock coat. See page 27.

Forage-Cap—blue cloth, with gold-embroidered peak, and band of gold lace an inch and three-quarters wide, of the staff pattern, in other respects as per sealed pattern for Staff Officers.

Great-Coat and Cape—as for General Officer, with regulation staff buttons. See page 18.

HORSE FURNITURE.

Saddle—hunting.

Saddle-Cloth—dark blue, of two feet ten inches in length and one foot ten inches in depth, with an edging of gold lace of the staff pattern, one inch wide, and the badges of a crown and star embroidered in silver on the corners.

Bridle—of black leather; bent branch bit with gilt bosses; the front and roses of garter blue.

Holsters—covered with black bearskin, except in tropical climates, when they are to be covered with black leather.

ADJUTANT-GENERAL
AND
QUARTER-MASTER-GENERAL,
WHEN HOLDING THE RANK OF GENERAL OFFICERS.

Coat—tunic, scarlet, with blue collar and cuffs; single-breasted, edged all round (except the collar) with round-back gold cord. On each side of the breast four loops of the same cord, with caps and drops, fastening with gold worked olivets, the top loop eight inches long, the bottom one four inches. On the back seams a gold cord, forming three eyes at the top, passing under a netted cap at the waist, below which it is doubled, and terminating in a knot at bottom of skirt. The skirt nine inches and a half deep, for an Officer of five feet nine inches, and half an inch variation for every inch of difference of height in the wearer, and lined with white, the bottom of skirt rounded off in front. The collar rounded off in front, laced round at top and bottom with inch gold oak-leaf lace, with a figure in gold braid between the laces, and the Officer's proper distinction as General, Lieutenant-General, or Major-General, embroidered in silver at each end; pointed cuff, ten and a half inches round, with a figure in gold inch oak-leaf lace and braid, upon the cuff and sleeve, extending eleven inches from the bottom of the cuff; according to sealed pattern deposited with Army Clothing Department.

Hat.
Loop.
Tassels.
Plume.
Stock.
Trousers.
Boots.
Spurs.
Sword and Scabbard.
Sword-Knot.
Sword-Belt and Plate.
Gloves.
} The same as a General Officer.

The sword-belt to be worn under the tunic and over the frock-coat.

Shoulder-Belt and Telescope-Case—According to a pattern deposited with Army Clothing Department, to be worn with tunic and blue frock.

Frock-Coat—blue, double-breasted, with rolling collar trimmed with three-quarter-inch black mohair lace; down the front on each side five loops of black Russian braid, with olivets, the top loop twelve inches and a half long, that at the waist seven and a quarter; plain pointed cuff, trimmed with black Russian braid forming a knot, which extends from edge of cuff to top, five inches and three-quarters; the skirt lined with black, and seventeen inches deep for an Officer five feet nine inches in height, with a variation of half an inch longer or shorter for each inch of difference in the height of the wearer. Sword-belt to be worn over the frock-coat.

Waistcoat—scarlet cloth, single-breasted, without collar, edged all round with gold Russian braid, and fastening down the front with hooks and eyes. To be worn with the blue frock-coat.

Trousers, Undress—Oxford mixture cloth, with a scarlet stripe down the outward seam, two inches and a half wide, and welted at the edges, and strapped as for cavalry, *see page* 84; to be worn with the blue frock coat only.

Forage-Cap—blue cloth, with gold embroidered peak, and band of gold oak-leaf lace, two inches wide, round the cap.

Great-Coat and Cape detached—blue cloth, the same as a General Officer. Page 18.

DEPUTY ADJUTANT-GENERAL
AND
DEPUTY QUARTER-MASTER-GENERAL,
WHEN HOLDING THE RANK OF GENERAL OFFICERS.

The same uniform as the Adjutant-General and Quarter-Master-General, excepting that the collar of the coat has a smaller figured braiding, and the figure upon the sleeve is smaller, extending only seven inches from the bottom of the cuff, as per pattern deposited with Army Clothing Department.

ADJUTANT-GENERAL
AND
QUARTER-MASTER-GENERAL,
IF UNDER THE RANK OF GENERAL OFFICERS.

Coat—tunic, scarlet, with blue collar and cuffs, single-breasted, edged all round (except the collar) with round-back gold cord. On each side of the breast four loops of the same cord, with caps and drops, fastening with gold worked olivets, the top loop eight inches long, the bottom one four inches. On the back seams a gold cord, forming three eyes at the top, passing under a netted cap at the waist, below which it is doubled, and terminating in a knot at bottom of skirt. The skirt as before described. The collar rounded off in front, and laced round the top and bottom with gold half-inch staff-pattern lace, with a rich figure in gold braid between the laces; the proper distinction of each Officer's rank, as Colonel or Lieutenant-Colonel, embroidered in silver at each end of the collar. Pointed cuff ten and a half inches round, with a rich figure in gold half-inch staff lace and braid on the cuff and sleeve, extending nine inches from the bottom of the cuff, as per sealed pattern, deposited with Army Clothing Department.

Hat—cocked, without binding; the fan, or back part, nine inches; the front seven and a half inches; each corner five inches; black ribbons on the two front sides.

Loop—of three-quarters of an inch gold lace, with regulation button (gilt, convex, frosted, the edge encircled with burnished laurel), and black silk cockade.

Tassels—flat netted purl head; gold crape fringe, an inch and five-eighths deep, with crimson crape fringe underneath.

Plume—of red and white upright swan feathers, five and a half inches long, from the stem to the end of the feathers, and the whalebone quite stiff.

Stock—black silk.

Trousers—blue cloth, with stripe of gold lace one inch and three-quarters, of the staff pattern, down the outward seam.

Boots—Wellington.

Spurs—screw, yellow metal, crane neck.

Sword—gilt three-quarter basket hilt, with device of sword and baton crossed; straight sabre blade, with rounded back, thirty-four inches long.

Scabbard—brass.

Sword-Knot—gold and crimson lace strap, with acorn tassel.

Sword-Belt—gold staff-pattern lace, an inch and a quarter wide, with sword carriages of the same, one inch wide; crimson morocco lining and edging. To be worn under the tunic and over the frock coat.

Plate—a round clasp, with V.R. and the crown on the centrepiece, and a wreath of laurel on the outer circle, all gilt.

Shoulder-Belt (*of gold staff-pattern lace, with crimson morocco lining and edging*) *and Telescope Case*— according to pattern deposited at Army Clothing Department, and to be worn with tunic and frock-coat.

Gloves—white leather.

Frock-Coat—blue, double-breasted, with rolling collar trimmed with three-quarter-inch black lace; down the front on each side five loops of black Russian braid, with olivets, the top loop twelve inches and a half long, that at the waist seven and a quarter; plain pointed cuff, trimmed with black Russian braid forming a knot, which extends from edge of cuff to top five inches and three-quarters; the skirt lined with black, and seventeen inches deep, for an Officer five feet nine inches in height, with a variation of half an inch longer or shorter for each inch of difference in the height of the wearer.

Trousers, Undress—Oxford mixture, but with red stripe of one and three-quarters inches wide, and strapped with leather as cavalry. See page 84.

Waistcoat—scarlet cloth, single-breasted, without collar, edged all round with gold Russian braid, and fastening down the front with hooks and eyes. To be worn with the blue frock-coat.

Forage-Cap—blue cloth, with gold-embroidered peak, and band of gold lace, an inch and three-quarters wide, of the staff pattern.

Great-Coat and detached Cape—as for General Officers, but with staff buttons.

DEPUTY ADJUTANT-GENERAL

AND

DEPUTY QUARTER-MASTER-GENERAL,

IF UNDER THE RANK OF GENERAL OFFICERS.

The same uniform as the Adjutant-General and Quarter-Master-General, when not a General Officer, except that the collar of the scarlet coat has a smaller figure in gold braid between the laces, and the figure upon the cuff and sleeve is smaller, extending only seven inches from the bottom of the cuff, as per sealed pattern, deposited with Army Clothing Department.

ASSISTANT ADJUTANT-GENERAL

AND

ASSISTANT QUARTER-MASTER-GENERAL.

Coat—as described for the Adjutant-General and Quarter-Master-General, if under the rank of General Officer, with the exception of the collar and sleeves. The collar is laced round with half-inch staff-pattern lace; a small figure in gold braid below the upper lace, and the proper Field Officer's badge in silver. The sleeves have a small figure in half-inch lace and braid, extending five inches and three-quarters from the bottom of the cuff, according to sealed pattern at Army Clothing Department.

DRESS OF STAFF OFFICERS. 29

The other articles of dress and equipment the same as for the Deputy Adjutant-General and Deputy Quarter-Master-General, when under the rank of General Officer.

DEPUTY-ASSISTANT ADJUTANT-GENERAL

AND

DEPUTY-ASSISTANT QUARTER-MASTER-GENERAL,

IF A FIELD OFFICER.

The same as an Assistant Adjutant-General or Assistant Quarter-Master-General, excepting that the collar has only an edging of braid within the laces, and the cuffs and sleeves have a smaller figure, of lace edged with braid, extending five inches and a quarter from the bottom of the cuff, according to sealed pattern at Army Clothing Department.

DEPUTY-ASSISTANT ADJUTANT-GENERAL

AND

DEPUTY-ASSISTANT QUARTER-MASTER-GENERAL,

IF NOT A FIELD OFFICER.

The same as a Deputy-Assistant, being a Field Officer, except that the collar is trimmed on the top only, with the proper badge of a Captain's or Subaltern's rank in silver. White patent leather pouch belt, and telescope case.

MAJOR OF BRIGADE.

The uniform and appointments of a Major of Brigade are the same as those of a Deputy-Assistant Adjutant-General.

HORSE FURNITURE
FOR
STAFF OFFICERS.

STAFF OFFICERS HOLDING THE RANK OF GENERAL OFFICERS
Are to adopt the horse furniture prescribed for their rank.

STAFF OFFICERS UNDER THE RANK OF GENERAL OFFICERS.

Saddle—hunting.

Saddle-Cloth—dark blue, of two feet ten inches in length, and one foot ten inches in depth, with an edging of gold lace (with beading of red cloth), of the staff pattern, one inch wide. If the Officer have the rank of Field Officer, his proper badge in silver (crown and star for Colonel, crown for lieutenant-Colonel, star for Major) on the corners; if below that rank, to have the edging of lace only.

Bridle—of black leather; bent branch bit, with gilt bosses, the front and roses of garter blue.

Holsters—covered with black bearskin, except in tropical climates, when they are to be covered with black patent leather.

Girths—white.

PERSONAL STAFF ATTACHED TO GENERAL OFFICERS.

MILITARY SECRETARY
TO THE
COMMANDER-IN-CHIEF.

If a General Officer, the uniform of his rank

MILITARY SECRETARIES
AND
ASSISTANT MILITARY SECRETARIES,
IF HOLDING THE RANK OF FIELD OFFICER.

Uniform and appointments the same as the Officers of the Adjutant-General's and Quarter-Master-General's departments, with the following exception :—

The collar of the scarlet coat is laced round the top and bottom with gold half-inch lace of the staff pattern, a vandyked figure in gold braid, according to pattern, between the laces, and at each end the badge of the Officer's rank is embroidered in silver. The cuff is edged with the same lace, and a vandyked figure, according to pattern, upon the cuff and sleeve, extends to nine inches and a half from the bottom of the cuff.

MILITARY SECRETARIES,
AND
ASSISTANT MILITARY SECRETARIES,
UNDER THE RANK OF A FIELD OFFICER.

The same uniform and appointments as Military Secretaries of Field Officers' rank, with the following exceptions:—

The collar is edged round the top only with round-back gold cord, under which is a vandyked figure in gold braid, according to pattern. The cuff is edged with the same cord, and the cuff and sleeve have a vandyked figure in gold braid, according to pattern, extending to seven inches and a half from the bottom of the cuff. White patent leather pouch belt and telescope case.

AIDES-DE-CAMP TO THE QUEEN.

DRESS.

Coat—tunic, scarlet; single-breasted, with eight gold embroidered frog-drop loops on each side, placed at equal distances, five of them, with buttons, above the waist, and three, without buttons, below it; each loop four inches long, exclusive of the drop. The coat to close down the front with hooks and eyes. Blue collar, rounded in front, with an embroidered frog-drop loop four inches long, exclusive of the drop at each end. Plain blue cuff; scarlet sleeve-flap, with three small buttons and embroidered frog-drop loops, one inch and three-quarters long, exclusive of the drops. Skirt twelve inches long, with variation before described, lined with white. Scarlet flaps on the skirts behind, ten inches long, and two inches wide at bottom; two buttons at the waist, and two on each flap, with embroidered frog-drop loops; the hind skirt and flaps, cuffs, and sleeve-flap, and top of the collar, edged with white.

Buttons—gilt, convex, with the Queen's cypher within a garter, and the crown over.

Aiguillette—gold, on the right shoulder. On the left shoulder, a gold cord.

Hat—cocked, without binding; the fan, or back part, nine inches; the front seven inches and a half; each corner five inches; black ribbons on the two front sides.

Loop—of three-quarter-inch gold lace, with regulation button, and black silk cockade.

Tassels—flat netted purl head; gold crape fringe, an inch and five-eighths deep, with crimson crape fringe underneath.

Plume—of red and white upright swan feathers five inches long from the stem to the end of the feathers, and the whalebone quite stiff.

Stock—black silk.

Trousers—blue cloth, with gold oak-leaf lace, one inch and three-quarters wide, down the outward seam.

Boots—Wellington.

Spurs—yellow metal, crane neck.

Sword—gilt three-quarter basket hilt, with device of sword and baton crossed; straight sabre blade, with rounded back, thirty-four inches long.

Scabbard—steel.

Sword-Knot—crimson and gold striped, acorn tassel.

Sword-Belt—Russia leather, with three stripes of gold embroidery; the carriages embroidered on both sides; the belt to be worn over the coat.

Plate—gilt, having the letters V.R., with the crown above, the motto "Dieu et mon droit" below, and an oak branch on each side, all in silver.

Sash—of the pattern worn by the Officers of the Foot Guards on state occasions.

Gloves—white leather

SCARLET UNDRESS.

Coat—as in *Dress*, except that the loops are of scarlet mohair cord straight across, instead of embroidery.

Aiguillette—as in *Dress*.

Trousers and all other articles of equipment as in *Dress*.

BLUE UNDRESS.

Frock-Coat—blue; single-breasted; stand-up cloth collar rounded in front, with one twist button-hole five inches long, and one small button at each end; eight buttons holes in the breast at equal distances, that at the top seven inches long, that at the waist three and a half inches; plain sleeve, with two holes and buttons; two buttons at the waist behind; plain flaps on skirt, with buttons at bottom. A small gold aiguillette on the right shoulder, and a gold cord on the left.

Trousers—Oxford mixture cloth, with a scarlet stripe down the outward seam, an inch and three-quarters wide, to be worn only with the blue frock-coat.

Forage-Cap—blue cloth, with gold embroidered peak, and band of gold oak-leaf lace, an inch and three-quarters wide. In all other respects as in *Dress*.

Great-Coat—as for Officers of the Staff under the rank of General Officer.

The principal Aide-de-Camp to Her Majesty, if holding the rank of a General Officer, is to wear the cocked hat and plume, sword and sword belt, sash, and button prescribed for his rank. His dress in other respects is to be similar to that of the Queen's Aides-de-Camp in general.

Her Majesty's Aides-de-Camp are to appear in full dress at drawing-rooms, court-balls, and on all state occasions, as well as at all reviews at which Her Majesty shall be present.

In the scarlet undress at levees, field days, and other military occasions when Her Majesty is present, unless specially ordered to the contrary.

Aides-de-Camp to Her Majesty, if on full pay of the Royal Artillery, are to wear a *blue* tunic, with scarlet collar, cuffs, and blue flaps, but in all other respects the uniform and appointments to be similar to that before described.

The embroidery, lace, tassels, sword knot, sword belt, sash, &c., of the MILITIA and YEOMANRY Aides-de-Camp are to be silver instead of gold. The scabbard to be steel.

HORSE FURNITURE
FOR
AIDES-DE-CAMP TO THE QUEEN.

Saddle—hunting.

Saddle-Cloth—of blue cloth, cut with a sweep behind, embroidered in the corners with V.R. in garter, with imperial crown at top, and oak foliage below, trimmed with two rows of gold lace, the outer row three-quarters of an inch wide, the inner row one inch wide, with a light of scarlet cloth between, a quarter of an inch wide.

Holsters—with petticoat bags, embroidered and trimmed to match; bear-skin tops.

Bridle—black leather, with chased gilt whole buckles; branch bit, with pads; shells on the cheeks, and water chain; gilt bosses, with V.R. in garter, and crown at top; blue front and roses.

Breastplate and Crupper—with gilt bosses.

AIDES-DE-CAMP TO GENERAL OFFICERS.

Coat—tunic scarlet, with blue collar and blue pointed cuffs, single-breasted, edged all round with round-back gold cord. On each side of the breast four loops of the same cord, with caps and drops, fastening with gold worked olivets; the top loop eight inches long, the bottom one four inches. On the back seams the same cord, forming three eyes at the top, passing under a netted cap at the waist, below which it is doubled, and terminating in a knot at bottom of skirt. The skirt nine inches and a half deep, with usual variation, and lined with white. The collar rounded off in front, and edged all round with gold cord, without other ornament or badge.

The army rank of the Officer is to be distinguished by the ornaments on the sleeve, cuff, and collar, as under :—

If a Subaltern, a knot of gold round-back cord and narrow braid, extending to seven inches and a half from the bottom of the cuff.

A Captain, the same knot edged with additional figures of narrow braid on the sleeve and cuff.

A Field Officer, a rich ornament of inch and a half lace and narrow braid on the sleeve and cuff, extending to eleven inches from the bottom of the cuff, and with relative badge on collar.

Hat—cocked, without binding; the fan or back part, nine inches; the front seven and a half inches each corner five inches; black ribbons on the two front sides.

Loop—of three-quarter inch gold lace, with regulation button,* and black silk cockade.

Tassels—flat netted purl head; gold crape fringe an inch and five-eighths deep, with crimson crape fringe underneath.

Plume—of red and white swan feathers, five and a half inches

---

* *i.e.* gilt, convex, frosted, with a raised crown in the centre.

long, from the stem to the end of the feathers, and the whalebone quite stiff.

Stock—black silk.

Trousers—blue cloth, with a stripe of gold lace one and three-quarter inches, of the staff pattern, down the outward seam.

Boots—Wellington.

Spurs—screw, yellow metal, crane neck, two inches long.

Gloves—white leather.

Sword—gilt three-quarter basket hilt, with device of sword and baton crossed; straight sabre-blade, with rounded back, thirty-four inches long.

Scabbard—steel.

Sword-Knot—gold and crimson lace strap, with acorn tassel.

Sword-Belt—Russia leather, with two stripes of gold embroidery; carriages embroidered on one side only. To be worn under the tunic and over the frock-coat.

Plate—gilt, having the letters V.R., with the crown above, the motto "Dieu et mon droit" below, and an oak branch on each side, all in silver. White patent leather pouch belt and telescope case.

Frock-Coat—blue; and *Waistcoat*—scarlet; of the patterns prescribed for the Officers of the Adjutant-General's and Quarter-Master-General's departments.

Trousers, undress—as for Staff Officers under the rank of Major-General, before given at page 27.

Forage-Cap—blue cloth, with gold-embroidered peak, and band of gold lace, an inch and three-quarters wide, of the staff pattern.

Great-Coat and Cape—as before directed for Staff Officers under the rank of Major-General.

HORSE FURNITURE

FOR

OFFICERS COMPOSING THE PERSONAL STAFF OF GENERAL OFFICERS.

MILITARY SECRETARY, IF A GENERAL OFFICER.

The Horse Furniture prescribed for his rank.

OFFICERS UNDER THE RANK OF GENERAL OFFICERS, AND EMPLOYED UPON THE PERSONAL STAFF OF GENERAL OFFICERS.

Saddle—hunting.

Saddle-Cloth—dark blue, of two feet ten inches in length, and one foot ten inches in depth, with an edging of gold lace, of the staff pattern, one inch wide, and with red cloth beading. Officers of the rank of Field Officer to have the badge of their rank embroidered in silver on the corners; below that rank, the edging of lace only.

Bridle—of black leather; bent branch bit, with gilt bosses; the front and roses of garter blue.

Holsters—covered with black bear-skin, except in tropical climates, when they are to be covered with black leather.

STAFF OF RECRUITING DISTRICTS AND INSPECTORS OF MILITIA.

INSPECTING FIELD OFFICERS
AND
INSPECTORS OF MILITIA.

Uniform and appointments the same as for a Colonel on the Staff, with the following exceptions:—

The badges on the collar to be according to each Officer's rank in the Army, crown and star for Colonel, crown for Lieutenant-Colonel, star for Major.

The buttons to be of the form and size prescribed for Infantry, with a raised crown and V.R.

ADJUTANT OF RECRUITING DISTRICTS
AND
SUB-INSPECTORS OF MILITIA.

Uniform and appointments the same as Inspecting Field Officer or Inspector of Militia, with the following exceptions:—

Coat—the collar, which has the proper badge of the Officer's rank in the Army at each end, is laced round the top only; the cuff has one row of lace; the edging of lace on

the sleeve and skirt flaps, and down the skirts behind, is omitted.
Blue Frock-Coat—without badge on the collar.
Scabbard—steel.

PAYMASTERS OF RECRUITING DISTRICTS.

The same dress as the Adjutant, without feather or sash.

STAFF OF GARRISONS.

GOVERNOR.

Coat— tunic, scarlet, single-breasted, with fly on inside one and three-quarter inches broad, and blue collar; the collar rounded off in front, and trimmed round top and bottom with half-inch lace; the cuff ten and a half inches round, two inches and a quarter deep, laced round the top with two rows of half-inch lace, leaving a light between; scarlet slashed flap on the sleeve six inches long, two and three-quarter inches wide, laced with half-inch lace and three loops of the same, with regulation buttons; nine buttons down the front at equal distances; the skirt $10\frac{1}{2}$ inches deep for an Officer of the height of five feet nine inches, with a variation of half an inch longer or shorter for every inch of difference in the height of the wearer; scarlet flap on the skirts behind, ten inches deep, edged with half-inch lace; two buttons on flap and one on waist, with three loops of half-inch lace, and the edges of the back-skirts behind laced with the same; the coat collar, cuffs, and flaps edged with white cloth quarter-inch, and the skirts lined with white.

Lace—gold, two-vellum pattern, half-inch width.

Buttons—Gilt, frosted, flat, with crown and portcullis in centre; the edge encircled with burnished laurel.

Hat—cocked, gold-lace loop, black silk cockade, regulation button, and tassels of gold crape fringe with crimson underneath.

Stock—black silk.

Trousers—blue cloth, with a stripe of gold lace one and three-quarter inches, staff pattern, down the outward seam.

Boots and Spurs—as for Officers of Infantry.

Sword—gilt three-quarter basket hilt, with device of sword and baton crossed; straight sabre blade, with rounded back, thirty-four inches long.

Scabbard—brass.

Sword-Knot—gold and crimson lace strap, with acorn tassel.

Sword-Belt—Russia leather, with two stripes of gold embroidery; carriages embroidered on one side only. To be worn over the coat.

Plate—gilt, having the letters V.R., with the crown above, the motto "Dieu et mon droit" below, and an oak branch on each side, all in silver.

Gloves—white leather.

Frock-Coat—blue; double-breasted, with stand-up cloth collar, cloth cuffs, and regulation buttons, according to Infantry pattern.

Forage-Cap—blue cloth, with gold-embroidered peak, and band of gold lace, an inch and three-quarters wide, of the same pattern as on the coat.

Great-Coat and Cape—as before described for Staff Officers under the rank of Major-General.

LIEUTENANT-GOVERNOR.

The same as for Governor, except that there is only one row of lace on the cuff and no lace on the bottom of the collar, nor on the edge of skirt flap and back skirt.

FORT OR TOWN MAJOR

Coat—the Infantry coat of his rank, with staff lace and buttons.

Hat—cocked, without binding; fan, or back part, nine inches; the front seven and a half inches; each corner five inches; black ribbons on the two front sides.

Loop—of three-quarter inch gold lace, with regulation button, and black silk cockade.

Tassels—flat netted purl head; gold crape fringe an inch and five-eighths deep, with crimson crape fringe underneath.

Plume—of red and white upright swan feathers, five and a half inches long, from the stem to the ends of the feathers, not joined or trimmed, and the whalebone quite stiff.

Stock—black silk.

Trousers—blue cloth, with a stripe of gold lace, as for other Staff Officers, down the outward seam.

Boots—Wellington.

Spurs—screw, yellow metal, crane neck, two inches long.

Sword—the same as for Officers of Infantry.

Scabbard—steel.

Sword-Knot—crimson and gold, with acorn tassel.

Sword-Belt—the same as for Officers of infantry.

Plate—gilt, with the words " Garrison Staff," and where there is a garrison badge, the device to be worn with the words " Garrison Staff " round it.

Sash—the same as for Officers of Infantry.

Gloves—white leather.

Frock-Coat—blue, according to the Infantry pattern, with staff buttons.

Trousers—Oxford mixture cloth, with a scarlet stripe down outward seam, one inch and three-quarters wide; to be worn with the blue frock-coat.

Forage-Cap—blue cloth, with gold-embroidered peak, and band of gold lace, an inch and three-quarters wide, of the staff pattern.

Great-Coat and Cape—as described for Infantry Officers.

FORT OR TOWN ADJUTANT.

The same as for *Town-Major*, page 43.

HORSE FURNITURE.

As prescribed for Staff Officers under the rank of General Officer, page 30.

ROYAL MILITARY COLLEGE.

GOVERNOR.

The same as for a General Officer, according to his rank.

LIEUTENANT-GOVERNOR, SUPERINTENDENT of STUDIES, CAPTAINS of COMPANIES, and ADJUTANT,

are to wear a uniform tunic, of the pattern prescribed for Infantry Officers of the Line, with blue cuffs and collar, gold lace of the two-vellum pattern, and buttons as for Colonel on the Staff; and the distinctions of rank according to their respective ranks in the army. The Lieutenant-Governor and Superintendent of Studies will wear a cocked hat with the plume as for Staff Officers, Captains of Companies a chaco, the Quarter-Master a cocked hat and corresponding infantry feathers. Trousers infantry pattern. Sword belt and plate as for Officers of Infantry, the plate bearing V.R. surmounted by crown.

THE RIDING-MASTER

is to wear the uniform prescribed for Light Dragoons according to his army rank.

THE MEDICAL OFFICERS

are to wear the uniform prescribed for their respective ranks.

ROYAL MILITARY ASYLUM.

Coat—tunic, scarlet, as prescribed for Officers of Infantry Regiments, with the proper distinctions of army rank.

Lace—gold, two-vellum pattern, half-inch width.

Buttons—gilt, flat, with a crown and V.R.

Hat—cocked; the fan, or back part, nine inches, the front seven inches and a half, each corner five inches; gold-lace loop, and tassels of gold-crape fringe, with crimson underneath.

Plume—red and white upright swan plume, five and a half inches long, from the ends of the feathers, and the whalebone quite stiff.

Trousers—blue cloth, with scarlet stripe, one inch and three-quarters wide, down the outward seam.

Sword—of the pattern prescribed for Officers of Infantry.

Scabbard—for the Commandant, brass; for the other Officers, black leather with gilt mountings.

Sword-Knot—as for Officers of Infantry.

Sword-Belt—black patent leather, with slings, and snake clasp, worn over the coat.

Sash—patent net crimson silk, with bullion-fringe ends worn over the left shoulder, but not to be worn by the Quarter-Master, or the Medical Officers; the latter to wear the small black feather prescribed for the Medical Staff of the army.

Blue Frock-Coat—as prescribed for Officers of Infantry.

CAVALRY DEPÔT.

The Officers of the several ranks to wear the uniform established for Regiments of Light Dragoons, with scarlet facings and gold lace. Sealed pattern of cap and sword belt plate deposited at Army Clothing Department.

HORSE FURNITURE.

Bridle and Saddle—as for other Cavalry Officers, but with bosses of staff pattern.

Shabracque—blue cloth, with a border of gold staff lace, one and a half inches wide, and of the pattern prescribed for Light Dragoons, having the open imperial crown with V.R. embroidered in gold in front and rear.

GARRISON OF CHATHAM.

COMMANDANT.

Uniform and appointments the same as for a Colonel on the Staff, with the proper badge of the Officer's army rank on the collar of tunic and frock coat.

STAFF CAPTAIN.

Uniform and appointments the same as the Commandant, with the following exceptions :

Coat—the collar, which has the Captain's badge of crown and star at each end, is laced round the top only; the cuffs have one row of lace, and the edging of lace on the sleeve and skirt flaps, and down the skirts behind, is omitted.

Scabbard—steel.

Spurs—(on occasions of mounted duty) steel, crane necked, two inches long.

The Paymaster and Adjutant to conform to the dress prescribed for Paymasters and Adjutants of Recruiting Districts.

HORSE FURNITURE.

Saddle—hunting.

Saddle-Cloth—dark blue, of two feet ten inches in length, and one foot ten inches in depth, with an edging of gold lace (and beading of red cloth) one inch wide, of the staff pattern. Officers of the rank of Field Officer to have their proper badge embroidered in silver on the corners.

Bridle—of black leather; bent branch bit, with gilt bosses; the front and roses of garter blue.

Holsters—covered with black bear-skin.

PROVISIONAL AND DEPÔT BATTALIONS.

The Field Officers of these battalions will wear the same uniform as Inspecting Field Officers of Recruiting Districts; their army rank being denoted by the distinctions on the collar of their coats, according to regulation. Horse furniture same as for Colonel on Staff, with the badge of Officer's rank on the saddle cloth.

The Adjutants (Captains) attached to these battalions will wear the uniform prescribed for Staff Captains in page 49, with steel scabbards and spurs.

The Medical Officers will wear the uniform of the Medical Staff of the Army, unless they belong to any Regiment, in which case they will wear their regimental uniform.

The Quarter-Masters, same as for Staff Captains, without collar badge, with the feather prescribed for Quarter-Masters of Infantry.

STAFF OFFICERS EMPLOYED IN THE PAYMENT AND ORGANIZATION OF OUT-PENSIONERS.

Coat—blue, double-breasted, with scarlet collar, lappels, and cuffs. The collar rounded off in front, lace and badges on collar according to rank. The lappels made to be worn either turned back or buttoned over. The cuff to be round, two inches and three-quarters deep, with one or two rows of half-inch lace, staff pattern, according to rank, round the top, the rows showing a light between. Width of sleeve at bottom ten inches and a half. Blue slashed flap on the sleeve, six inches long and two inches and a quarter wide, laced at the edge for Field Officers, but plain under that rank, with three buttons and loops of half-inch lace. On the left shoulder a crimson silk cord to retain the sash, with a small button. Two rows of buttons down the front, nine in each row at equal distances, the distance between the rows eight inches at top and four at bottom; waist long. The skirt $10\frac{1}{2}$ inches deep for an Officer five feet nine inches in height, with a variation of half an inch longer or shorter for each inch of difference in the height of the wearer. Blue flap on the skirts behind, ten inches deep; two buttons on flap and one on waist, with three loops of lace.

The edge of the flap and edges of the back skirts to be laced with half-inch lace for Field Officers, plain under that rank. The coat, collar, cuffs, and flaps not edged, the skirts to be lined with black silk.

Lace—gold, staff pattern, half inch wide.

Buttons—gilt, convex, frosted, the edge encircled with burnished laurel.

Hat—cocked, without binding; the fan, or back part, nine inches, the front seven and a half inches, each corner five inches; black ribbons on the two front sides.

Loop—of three-quarter inch gold lace, with regulation button and black silk cockade.

Tassels—flat netted purl head; gold crape fringe, an inch and five-eighths deep, with crimson crape fringe underneath.

Plume—of red and white upright swan feathers, five and a half inches long from the stem to the ends of the feathers, and the whalebone quite stiff.

Stock—black silk.

Trousers—Oxford mixture cloth, with scarlet stripe one inch and three quarters broad down outward seam.

Boots—Wellington.

Spurs—screw, straight neck, two inches long, yellow metal for Field Officers, steel under that rank.

Sword—gilt, three-quarter basket hilt, with device of sword and baton crossed; straight sabre blade, with rounded back, thirty-four inches long.

Scabbard—brass for Field Officers, steel under that rank.

Sword-Knot—gold and crimson lace strap, with acorn tassel.

Sword-Belt—Russia leather, with two stripes of gold embroidery; carriages embroidered on one side only; to be worn over the coat.

Plate—gilt, having the letters V. R., with the crown above, the motto "Dieu et mon droit" below, and an oak branch on each side, all in silver.

Sash—crimson silk net, with fringe ends, united by a crimson runner, worn diagonally over the left shoulder. The ends of the fringe not to hang lower than the bottom of the coat.

Gloves—white leather.

Forage-Cap—blue cloth, with gold-embroidered peak, and band of gold lace, an inch and three-quarters wide, of the staff pattern, gold button and braid on top, as for Staff Officers.

Great-Coat and Cape—as for Staff Officers under the rank of General Officer.

MEMORANDUM.

The Officers are permitted to wear the forage cap with the tunic for the sake of uniformity, as the pensioners have only a forage cap.

MEDICAL STAFF CORPS.

As Staff Captain, page 49.

PROVOST MARSHAL.

Coat—tunic, scarlet, according to the regulation for Subalterns of Infantry, but the collar without any device; plain gilt buttons, lace of the two-vellum pattern

Hat—cocked; the fan, or back part, nine inches, the front seven inches and a half, each corner five inches; gold-lace loop, three-quarters of an inch wide; gold roses; no feather.

Trousers—blue cloth, with a scarlet stripe one and three-quarter inches wide down the outer seam.

Sword—the same as for Officers of Infantry.

Scabbard—black leather with gilt mountings.

Sword-Belt
Sash
Stock } The same as for Officers of Infantry.
Boots
Gloves

Cloak—blue cloth, lined with scarlet, according to pattern prescribed for Officers of Infantry.

Blue Frock Coat, the same as for Subalterns of Infantry.

CIVIL DEPARTMENTS.

MEDICAL.

Coat—tunic, scarlet, single-breasted, with black velvet collar, cuffs, and sleeve flaps. The collar rounded off in front, cuff ten and a half inches round, two inches and three-quarters deep. Slashed flap on the sleeve six inches long and two inches and a quarter wide, with three loops of half-inch lace and uniform buttons. Eight buttons down the front. The skirt $10\frac{1}{2}$ inches deep for an Officer of five feet nine inches in height, with a variation of half an inch longer or shorter for every inch of difference in the height of the wearer. Scarlet flap on the skirt behind, ten inches deep, two buttons on flap and one on waist, with three loops of half-inch lace. The coat, collar, cuffs, and flaps edged with white cloth a quarter of an inch broad, and the skirts lined with white.

Director-General, Army Medical Department—as Major-General. Collar, cuffs, sleeve slashes, and skirt-flaps, to be laced with inch lace (staff pattern) as directed for Major-General.

Distinctions of Rank—according to the relative ranks in the army, viz. :—

Inspector-General of Hospitals, as Brigadier-General. The collar laced round top and bottom with half-inch lace ; a crown and star embroidered in silver at each end.

Deputy Inspector-General of Hospitals, as Lieutenant-Colonel, the same lace, with a crown at end of the collar.

Staff-Surgeon of the First Class, as Major, the same lace, with a star at each end of collar.

Staff-Surgeon of the Second Class, as Captain, the top only of the collar laced with half-inch lace, and a crown and star in silver at each end.

Assistant Staff-Surgeon, as Lieutenant, the same collar, with a crown at each end.

The Officers ranking with Field Officers to have two rows of half-inch lace round the top of the cuff, an edging of the same on the sleeve and skirt flaps, and down the edge of the skirt behind.

The Officers under that rank to have one row of lace round the cuff, none on the skirt, and the loops only on the skirt flap and sleeve flap.

Lace—gold, two-vellum pattern, half-inch width.

Buttons—gilt, with the crown and letters V.R., with the words "Medical Staff" within a star raised thereon.

Hat—cocked, plain; the fan, or back part, nine inches, the front seven inches and a half, each corner five inches.

Loop—scale, with regulation button, and black silk cockade.

Tassels—gold bullion.

Feather—black cock's tail, drooping from a feathered stem three inches in length.

Stock—black silk.

Trousers, Dress—blue cloth, with gold lace two and a half inches wide for Director-General, and an inch and three-quarters wide for Officers below that rank, down outward seam.

Boots—Wellington.

Spurs—screw, yellow metal, as for Staff Officers, for those Medical Officers who are allowed forage for a horse.

Sword—the same as for Officers of Infantry.

Scabbard—brass for those having the rank of Field Officer, black leather, with gilt mountings, for Officers under that rank.

Sword-Knot—crimson and gold, with acorn tassel.

Sword-Belt—black morocco, with three rows of gold embroidery for Director-General; two rows for Inspector-

General of Hospitals; black leather, with slings and gilt hook for all other ranks. To be worn over the coat.

Plate—a round gilt clasp, with V.R. surmounted by a crown, in silver, upon the centre-piece, and "Medical Staff" with a laurel branch, also in silver, on the outer circle.

Shoulder-Belt—black morocco, with three rows of gold embroidery for Director-General, with two rows for Inspector-General of Hospitals, and black patent leather for all other ranks; the whole with a small case of surgical instruments, according to pattern.

Frock-Coat—blue, double-breasted, with stand-up collar rounded off in front, cuffs, and lappels all of blue cloth.* Cuff, ten and a half inches round, and two inches and three-quarters deep, slashed flap on sleeve five inches and a quarter long, one inch and a half wide, with three small uniform buttons. Two rows of uniform buttons down the front, nine in each row, at equal distances, the distance between the rows eight inches at top, and four inches at bottom; flaps on skirts behind ten inches deep, with two buttons on flap and one on waist. The skirt lined with black, and seventeen inches deep for an Officer five feet nine inches in height, with a variation of half an inch longer or shorter for each inch of difference in the height of the wearer. The Officers ranking with Field Officers to have the badge of their rank (as crown or star) embroidered in gold at each end of the collar. The collars of other officers to be plain.

Trousers, Undress—blue cloth, with a scarlet stripe two and a half inches wide down the outward seam for Director-General, one and three-quarter inches for Inspector-General of Hospitals, and scarlet welt for all other ranks.

Boots—Wellington or ankle.

---

* Collar and cuffs of blue velvet for Director-General, with star in gold embroidery at each end of the collar.

Forage-Cap—Director-General as for Major-General, except that the band is to be of lace, of the staff pattern. The same for Inspector-General of Hospital, gold button and trimming on the top. For all other ranks, blue cloth, with black leather peak and chin strap; black silk oak-leaf band, with V.R., surmounted by a crown, embroidered in gold on the front, and with black button and trimming.

Great-Coat—of Infantry pattern, blue cloth, lined with scarlet, with uniform buttons.

Officers of the Medical Department, serving in Africa, are to wear the shell jacket as prescribed for Officers of Infantry.

Horse Furniture—bridle, as Officers of Infantry, with black leather front and rosettes. Bit, without bosses. Saddle-cloth for Officers who are allowed forage for a horse, blue cloth, same dimensions as for Infantry Officers, with the lace of black silk, one inch wide. Holsters, covered with black leather. Girths, blue. Saddle, hunting.

Purveyor-in-Chief - - - with rank of Major.
Purveyor of Hospitals and Apothecary „ Captain.
Deputy Purveyor „ Lieutenant.

The above to wear the same uniform and appointments as the Officers of the Commissariat Department of corresponding rank, except the facings and edgings, which are to be of grey cloth.

Medical and Purveyors' Clerks on the establishment to wear only a frock-coat similar to that of a Deputy Purveyor; with this difference, that they are not to wear the embroidered V.R. on the Forage Cap. The trousers to be blue without welt. Sword and belt as for Deputy Purveyor.

COMMISSARIAT.

Coat—tunic, blue, single-breasted, with black velvet collar, cuffs, and slash on sleeve. The collar rounded off in front, cuff round, two and three-quarter inches deep, and ten and a half round; slashed flap on sleeve six inches long and two and a quarter inches wide, with three loops of half-inch lace, staff pattern, and uniform buttons. Eight buttons in front, at equal distances. The skirt 10½ inches deep for an Officer five feet nine inches in height, with a variation of half an inch longer or shorter, for every inch of difference in the height of the wearer. Blue flap on the skirt behind, ten inches deep, two buttons on flap, and one on waist, with three loops of half-inch lace. The coat, collar, cuffs, and flaps edged with white cloth, quarter-inch, and the skirts lined with white.

Distinctions of Rank—according to the relative ranks in the army, viz. :—

Commissary-General—as Brigadier-General, the collar laced round the top and bottom, a crown and star embroidered in silver at each end.

Deputy Commissary-General of three years' standing—as Lieutenant-Colonel, the same lace, with a crown at each end of the collar.

Deputy Commissary-General under three years—as Major, the same lace, with a star.

Assistant Commissary-General—as Captain, lace round the top only of the collar; a crown and star in silver at each end.

Deputy Assistant Commissary-General—as Lieutenant, the same lace, with a crown.

Clerk, Established—as Ensign, the same lace, with a star.

The Officers ranking with Field Officers to have two rows of half-inch lace round the top of the cuff, an edging of the same on the sleeve and skirt flaps, and down the edge of the skirts behind.

The Officers under that rank to have one row of lace round the cuff, none on the skirt, and the loops only on the skirt and sleeve flaps.

Buttons—gilt, with the crown and star, and the "Commissariat Staff" raised thereon.

Hat—cocked ; the fan, or back part, nine inches, the front seven inches and a half, each corner five inches ; uniform button, gold-lace loop, and tassels of good crape fringe, with crimson underneath.

Stock—black silk.

Trousers—blue cloth, with a gold stripe one and three-quarter inches wide, staff pattern, down the outward seam.

Boots—Wellington.

Spurs—steel, crane neck, two inches long.

Sword—the same as for Officers of Infantry.

Scabbard—brass, for Officers ranking as Field Officers, steel for all other ranks.

Sword-Knot—crimson and gold, with acorn tassel.

Sword-Belt—black morocco, with two rows of gold embroidery for Commissary-General; black leather, with slings and gilt hook, for all other ranks. To be worn over the coat.

Plate—a round gilt clasp, with V.R. surmounted by a crown, in silver, upon the centre piece, and "Commissariat Staff," with a laurel branch, also in silver, on the outer circle.

Gloves—white leather.

Frock-Coat—blue, double-breasted, with stand-up collar rounded off in front; cuffs and lappels all blue. Cuff, ten and a half inches round, and two and three-quarter inches deep, slashed flap on sleeve five and a quarter inches long and one and a half inches wide, with three small uniform buttons. Two rows of uniform buttons down the front, nine in each row at equal distances, the distance between the rows eight inches at top and four inches at bottom; flaps on skirts behind ten inches deep, with two buttons on flap, and one on waist; the skirt lined with black, and seventeen inches deep for an Officer five feet nine inches in height, with a variation of half an inch longer or shorter for each inch of difference in the height of the wearer. The Officers ranking with Field Officers to have the badge of their rank (as crown or star) embroidered in gold at each end of the collar. The collars of other Officers to be plain.

Undress Trousers—plain blue.

Boots—Wellington or ankle.

Forage-Cap—for Commissary-General as for Inspector-General of Hospitals; blue cloth, with black leather peak and chinstrap; black silk oak-leaf band, with V.R. surrounded by a wreath, surmounted by a crown, embroidered in gold on the front, with black button and trimming on the top for all other ranks.

Shell-Jacket—blue, black velvet collar, and pointed cuffs five inches deep, 10 buttons down the front at equal distances.

Cloak—blue, lined with scarlet, of pattern for Officers of Infantry, with uniform buttons.

Horse Furniture—as for Medical Officers.

JUDGE ADVOCATE.

Coat—tunic, scarlet; according to the pattern prescribed for Officers of Infantry below the rank of Field Officer, without badge upon the collar.

Lace—gold, two-vellum pattern.

Button—gilt, with the crown and letters V.R., of the same pattern as fixed for the Staff of Recruiting Districts.

Hat—cocked, plain; the fan, or back part, nine inches; the front, seven inches and a half; each corner, five inches; black button and black silk loop.

Stock—black silk.

Trousers—blue cloth.

Boots—Wellington.

Sword—the same as for Officers of Infantry.

Scabbard—black leather, with gilt mountings.
Sword-Knot—crimson and gold, with acorn tassel.
Sword-Belt—black leather, to be worn over the coat.
Gloves—white leather.
Frock-Coat—blue, with uniform buttons.

If a Military Officer, the unattached uniform according to his rank in the army.

DRESS FOR GENERAL OFFICERS OF HUSSARS.

TO BE WORN WHEN SPECIALLY SANCTIONED BY HER MAJESTY.

Tunic—Entirely of blue cloth, single-breasted; the collar rounded in front, and ornamented with three-quarter inch gold lace (oak-leaf pattern) and gold braid, having a rich oak-leaf figure in braiding between the two. On each side of the breast six loops of gold chain lace, with caps and drops, fastening with six gold worked olivets; the top loop eight inches long, the bottom one four inches. The jacket edged all round (except the collar) with gold chain lace. On the back seams, a double chain of the same lace edged with braid, forming three eyes at top, passing under a netted cap at the waist, and terminating in a knot at bottom of skirt. The skirt nine inches deep for an Officer of five feet nine inches in height, with the usual variation according to the difference in height of the wearer. Skirt lined with black. Sleeve; a knot of gold chain lace, edged with gold braiding (oak leaf figure), the whole extending from edge of cuff to top, eleven inches. The relative badge on collar.

Trousers—blue cloth, with a stripe of gold lace, of the pattern and width established for other General Officers, down the outward seam.

Sword—as for Officers of Hussars.

Sword-Knot—ditto.

Sword-Belt—as for General Officers.

Sabretache—scarlet cloth face, laced with gold lace two inches and a quarter wide (oak-leaf pattern), leaving an edge of scarlet; gold embroidered V.R. and Imperial crown, with sword and baton encircled with wreath of laurel underneath; three gilt rings at top. Pocket, scarlet morocco.

Pouch-Belt—gold lace, one inch and a half wide, oak-leaf pattern. Scarlet cloth edging; gilt ornamented buckle tip and slide, attached to sides of pouch. For Dress and Undress.

Pouch-Box—same as for Officers of Hussars; with cross, sword, and baton, in wreath of laurel, surmounted by Imperial crown, embroidered in gold.

UNDRESS.

Frock-Coat—same as for Colonels of Hussars, with relative collar badge.

Trousers—blue cloth with red stripes, as for General Officers; strapped with patent leather, as directed for Officers of Cavalry.

Forage-Cap—as for Officers of Hussars, with gold lace braid as for General Officers.

Great-Coat and Cape—as for General Officers.

HORSE FURNITURE.

Bridle—bit and bosses as for General Officers, head-stall, reins, and throat-drop as for Officers of Hussars.

Saddle—as for Officers of Cavalry.

Shabracque—blue cloth, of the dimensions prescribed for Officers of Hussars, trimmed with two rows of gold oak-leaf lace inch and a half wide, showing a light between; and to bear in the hind corners the ornaments embroidered in silver, as follows:—

For a *General Officer*—crown and star.

    Lieut.-General—crown.

    Major-General—star.

The front corners to bear initials V.R. surmounted by Imperial crown embroidered in gold.

DRESS OF OFFICERS

OF

REGIMENTS OF CAVALRY.

LIFE GUARDS. } Dress and Horse
ROYAL REGIMENT OF HORSE GUARDS. } Furniture.

DRAGOON GUARDS AND HEAVY DRAGOONS.

LIGHT DRAGOONS.

HUSSARS.

LANCERS.

HORSE FURNITURE FOR OFFICERS OF ALL CAVALRY REGIMENTS (*The Household Brigade excepted*).

MILITARY TRAIN.

OFFICERS

OF

REGIMENTS OF CAVALRY.

The Blue Frock-Coat, as prescribed for the Officers of the Cavalry, may be worn with the forage-cap, as a common morning riding-dress in quarters; but at all drills or parades, when the men appear in their stable-dress, or drill order, the Officers of Dragoon Guards and Heavy Dragoons will appear in the *Stable-Jacket*, which may also be worn at the regimental mess.

When Regimental Officers attend in uniform, as spectators, the review or inspection of troops by the Commander-in-Chief, or by any General Officer, they are to appear in the uniform of their respective regiments, and not in the blue Frock-coat.

Officers in mourning, when dressed in uniform, are to wear a piece of black crape round the left arm, above the elbow.

Officers and non-commissioned Officers of Cavalry are permitted to wear a plain black leather sabretache, as an article of field equipment, but not to be worn on other than mounted duties. The sabretache is not to hang below the calf of the leg. Sealed patterns are deposited at Army Clothing Department.

The lace of Officers of Yeomanry to be of silver, and the distinctive collar badges are to be embroidered in gold.

The distinctions of regimental badges and devices, and other peculiar distinctions which may have been granted under special authority to different regiments of Cavalry, are to be preserved.

FIRST LIFE GUARDS.

DRESS.

Coat—tunic, scarlet, with blue velvet collar, and edged round with blue cloth, single-breasted, with nine regimental buttons in front at equal distances, collar embroidered and rounded off in front, with distinction badges of rank, gauntlet cuff of blue velvet, with embroidered loop and button, two buttons at waist and three loops of embroidery on each skirt, the skirts nine inches long, for an Officer five feet nine inches in height, (with the usual variation,) lined with blue, and rounded off in front.

The Field Officers distinguished by a row of embroidery round top of collar and cuffs.

The several ranks to be distinguished as follows :—
    Colonel—Crown and Star of the Garter, in silver, at each end of the collar with embroidery.
    Lt.-Colonel—Crown and embroidery.
    Major—Star and embroidery.
    Captain—Crown and Star.
    Lieutenant—Crown.
    Sub-Lieutenant—Star.

Embroidery—of gold, oak-leaf pattern.

Aiguillette and Shoulder-Strap—of twisted gold cord, with gilt engraved tags, worn on the right shoulder; a gold twist cord strap similar to that of the aiguillette worn on the left shoulder.

Helmet—German silver mounted, with gilt ornaments, and silver Garter star in front.

Plume—of white horsehair.
Stock—black silk.
Pantaloons—of white leather.
Boots—jacked.
Spurs—steel, with chains and buckles.
Sword—half basket, steel pierced hilt, with regimental cypher in brass, the edges of basket ornamented with twelve plain brass studs; lining of white leather, back piece of plain polished steel, with a brass cap; straight cut-and-thrust blade, and full one inch broad at shoulder, thirty-nine inches long, extreme length, forty-five inches.
Scabbard—steel, with plain brass mountings.
Sword-Knot—crimson and gold, with leather strap.
Sword-Belt—gold lace with enamelled plate, with star and crown, double cypher of L.G., with a scroll bearing the words "Peninsula," "Waterloo."
Pouch-Belt—gold lace, with gilt mountings, and red silk cord down centre.
Pouch—black patent leather, with gilt mountings.
Gloves—white patent leather gauntlets.
Cuirass—steel, ornamented with brass studs, edging blue silk velvet; scales gilt, with gold and velvet ends; straps blue morocco leather and gold, buckle gilt.
Trousers—blue cloth, with a stripe of gold lace, two inches and a half wide, down the outward seam.
Boots—ankle.
Spurs—gilt, crane neck.

UNDRESS.

Frock-Coat—blue, single-breasted, hook and eye, stand-up collar, rounded off with figured pattern, with six loops of three-quarter inch braid in front, and four rows of olivets, seven-eighths braid on edge down arms and side seams, eyes and fringe at hips, with tassels; trimmed cuffs extending twelve inches up sleeves. Field Officers to wear the relative badges on the collar.
Stable-Jacket—scarlet, round, single-breasted, hook and eye studs up front, collar blue velvet, rounded, with half-inch

oak-leaf lace round top, cuffs of blue velvet pointed five inches deep with lace, like collar, on each shoulder a gold cord and button. Field Officers to wear the relative badges on collar.

Trousers—blue cloth, with two scarlet stripes, each an inch and a half wide, down the outward seam, leaving a light between the seam, welted with scarlet cloth.

Spurs—steel.

Sword and Scabbard—with the undress uniform the same as with dress.

Sword-Knot—white leather.

Sword-Belt—white patent leather, two inches wide, fastening in front, with two inch and a quarter gilt plate, with star and crown, double cypher of L.G., with a scroll bearing the words "Peninsula," "Waterloo."

Pouch-Belt—white patent leather, with gilt mountings.

Pouch—same as dress.

Forage-Cap—blue cloth, with a scarlet welt round the top, scarlet band, peak embroidered in dead and bright gold, a buckle and strap, according to regimental pattern.

Gloves—white leather.

Cloak—red, blue cape and collar, and gold lace one inch and a quarter on the ends of collar.

REGIMENTAL STAFF.

The Adjutant and Riding Master are to wear the uniform of their rank.

Coat, tunic—The Quarter-Master, Surgeon, Assistant-Surgeon, and Veterinary-Surgeon, wear the same as other Officers, with aiguillette and shoulder strap.

Hat—cocked, the Quarter-Master wears regimental looping, tassel and a feather, the Surgeon, Assistant-Surgeon, and Veterinary-Surgeon have a black silk loop, no feather.

Appointments and other articles of dress the same as worn by the other officers of the regiment.

HORSE FURNITURE.

FIRST LIFE GUARDS.

Saddle-Cloth—blue; forty-one inches long and twenty-nine inches deep, fore and hind corners pointed, laced round with three rows of gold lace, the centre row of lace two and a half inches wide; the side pieces five-eighths of an inch wide, with a scarlet quarter of an inch light between the laces; the lace to be oak-leaf pattern, embroidered on hind corner with crown and scrolls, "Waterloo" and "Peninsula," and reversed cypher L. G., a small number one over it, all gold, a garter star underneath, proper, also petticoat bags twenty-three inches deep, fourteen and a half inches wide, laced the same as saddle cloth, embroidered with crown, number one, and reversed L. G., all gold on blue cloth, with bearskin caps.

Seat-Cover—doe-skin.

Saddle—high mounting saddle with brass cantle, shoe cases. A white leather cover for dress.

Holsters—brown holsters and patent leather straps.

Stirrup-Leathers—brown, made up plain

Stirrups—large, square set, steel.

Ditto, dress—brass, engraved oak-leaf pattern.

Slides and Tips—steel, with brass studs.

Girths—white linen web.

Surcingle—patent leather.

Ditto—for dress, white web.

Bridle—patent leather, with brass whole buckles, chain head piece and front, with bosses at each end, star centre.

Collar—patent leather.

Chain—brass.

Bit—steel, with bar and water chain, Russian hooks and steel loops, for cheek of bridle, brass bosses with crown and regimental cypher.

Bridoon—link and tee.

NOTE.—Patterns of all bosses for all ranks and regiments are deposited at the Army Clothing Department.

Breastplate—patent leather, brass whole buckles, and boss.
Crupper—turn back, with brass boss.
Shabracque—undress, bearskin.

SECOND LIFE GUARDS.

REGULATIONS FOR THE DRESS OF THE OFFICERS.

DRESS.

Tunic—scarlet, edged round with blue velvet, single-breasted, nine regimental buttons in front at equal distances, blue velvet collar embroidered and rounded off in front, with distinction badges of rank ; gauntlet cuff of blue velvet, with embroidered loop and button, two buttons at waist, and three loops of embroidery on each skirt, the skirt nine inches long, for an Officer five feet nine inches in height, (with the usual variation,) lined with drab silk, and rounded off in front.

The Field Officers distinguished by a row of embroidery round top of collar and cuffs.

The several ranks to be distinguished as under :—
Colonel—a crown and star of the garter in silver at each end of the collar, with embroidery.
Lieut.-Colonel—the crown and embroidery.
Major—the star and embroidery.
Captain—the crown and star.
Lieutenant—the crown.
Sub.-Lieut.—the star.
Embroidery—gold oak-leaf pattern.
Aiguillette and Shoulder Strap—of twisted gold cord, with gilt engraved tags worn on the right shoulder, a gold twist cord strap similar to that of the aiguillette worn on the left shoulder.

SECOND LIFE GUARDS.

Helmet—German silver, mounted with gilt ornaments, and Garter star in front.
Plume—white horse hair.
Stock—black silk.
Pantaloons—white leather.
Boots—jacked.
Spurs—steel, with straps and buckles.
Sword—gilt, half-basket hilt guard, pommel, and shell, black fish-skin gripe, with gilt twisted wire, straight steel cut-and-thrust blade, thirty-nine inches long, and full one inch broad at shoulder, extreme length forty-five inches.
Scabbard—steel, with brass mountings.
Sword-Knot—crimson and gold, with embroidered leather strap.
Sword-Belt—gold oak-leaf lace, two inches wide, on morocco leather, with two gold-laced slings, gilt plate in front, with enamelled silver Garter star.
Pouch-Belt—gold oak-leaf lace, two and a half inches wide, on morocco leather, gilt plain buckle, tip and slide, blue silk cord down centre of belt.
Pouch—black patent leather, with gilt ornament, bearing a silver enamelled Garter star in centre.
Gloves—white patent leather gauntlets.
Cuirass—back and front of polished steel, with brass studs, bound with blue morocco leather, edged with blue velvet, and lined throughout with red morocco leather; scales, double gilt, lined with blue morocco leather; straps, gold lace, oak leaf pattern, with gilt buckle, and gold embroidered buckle shade.
Trousers—blue cloth, with a stripe of oak-leaf gold lace two and a half inches wide down the outward seam.
Boots—ankle.
Spurs—gilt, crane neck.

UNDRESS.

Frock-Coat—blue single breasted, hook and eye, stand-up collar, rounded off and ornamented with braid, six loops of three-quarter inch braid in front, and four rows of olivets, seven-eighths braid on edge down arm and side seams, eyes and fringe at hips, with tassels, pointed cuffs extending twelve inches up sleeves, with relative badges on collar for F. O.

Stable-Jacket—scarlet, edged with blue velvet, round single breasted, hook and eye studs up front; collar, blue velvet, rounded, half-inch oak-leaf lace round top; cuffs of blue velvet, pointed five inches deep with lace, as on collar; a gold cord and button on each shoulder, with relative badges on collar for F. O.

Trousers—blue cloth with two scarlet stripes one inch wide, and cord between down the outward seams.

Boots—ankle.

Spurs—steel.

Sword and Scabbard—same as dress.

Sword-Knot—white buff leather.

Sword-Belt—white patent leather, two inches wide, fastening in front with a gilt plate same as dress; two sword-slings one inch wide.

Pouch-Belt—white patent leather, with gilt buckles, and blue silk cord down centre.

Pouch-box—same as dress.

Forage-Cap—oilskin, with gold embroidered peak, according to regimental pattern.

Gloves—white leather.

Cloak—scarlet cloth, with blue collar and cape.

REGIMENTAL STAFF.

The Adjutant and Riding Master wear the uniform of their rank.

Coat—The Quarter-Master, Surgeon, Assistant-Surgeon, and Veterinary Surgeon wear the same as the other Officers, with aiguillette and shoulder strap.

Hat—cocked. The Quarter-Master wears regimental looping, tassels and feather; the Surgeon, Assistant-Surgeon, and

Veterinary Surgeons have a black silk loop and no feather.

Appointments and other articles of dress the same as those worn by the other Officers of the regiment.

HORSE FURNITURE.

SECOND LIFE GUARDS.

Shabracque—blue; forty-eight inches long, thirty-two inches deep, fore and hind corners rounded, with a scarlet border inserted round the shabracque, four and three-quarter inches wide, inserted one and a quarter inches from edge of shabracque on which scarlet border to be placed; gold oak-leaf lace, two and a half inches wide, three-quarters of an inch from outer edge of scarlet, embroidered on fore and hind corners, a lion and crown, the scrolls " Waterloo " and " Peninsula " with laurel leaves enclosing a garter, star, and number two, on hind corners only, the star proper and the rest in gold.

Saddle—with fan tails, brass cantle, and fittings for shoe cases.

Horse-shoe Cases—a pair of brown leather.

Girth—white linen web.

Stirrup-leather—brown, plain and steel buckles.

Stirrups—oval pattern, steel.

Slides—brass, steel centres.

Holsters—brown; with holster and cloak strap in one.

Bridle—plain black leather, brass buckles, a brass scale head piece, with white buff front for dress.

Bridle bit—steel, with bar, boss same as breastplate.

Collar—black leather brass furniture.

Chain—steel.

Bridoon—link and tee.

Gold ditto—gold lace bridoon, head and rein for dress with ring bridoon.

Breastplate—black plain leather with brass boss; Queen's crest, encircled with the words "Peninsula and Waterloo."
Breastplate, dress—patent leather with silver garter star.
Crupper—turnback, with boss, the same as on breastplate.
Surcingle—brown leather retaining strap.
Undress Shabracque—black lambskin.
Valise—blue cloth, twenty-four inches long, six and a half inch ends, 2. L. G., embroidered in gold.

ROYAL HORSE GUARDS.

REGULATIONS FOR THE DRESS OF THE OFFICERS.

Coat—tunic, blue, edged throughout with scarlet cloth, single-breasted, nine regimental buttons down the front; scarlet cloth collar and cuffs; collar embroidered at each end with an oak-leaf loop, five and a half inches long and two inches deep; a similar loop on the cuff, with a regimental button in the centre; skirts nine inches deep, for an Officer five feet nine inches in height (with usual variation) open behind, with three embroidered loops on each side, drooping downwards; two buttons on the waist at back; skirts lined with scarlet cassimere, and rounded off in front.

The field officers to have a row of embroidery round the collar and cuffs, three quarters of an inch deep.

The several ranks to be distinguished as under:—

Colonel—a crown and star of the garter, in silver, at each end of the collar, with embroidery.
Lieut.-Colonel—the crown and embroidery.
Major—the star and embroidery.
Captain—the crown and star.

Lieutenant—the crown.
Cornet—the star.
Embroidery—gold, oak leaf pattern.
Aiguillette—twisted gold cord, with shoulder-strap, and gilt engraved tags, worn on the right shoulder; a gold twist cord strap, similar to that of the aiguillette, worn on the left shoulder.
Helmet—German silver, mounted with gilt ornaments, and silver garter star in front.
Plume—red horse hair.
Stock—black silk.
Pantaloons—white leather.
Boots—jacked.
Spurs—steel, with straps and buckles.
Sword—gilt guard, pommel, and shell; black fish skin gripe twisted with yellow wire, straight cut-and-thrust blade, full one inch wide at shoulder, blade thirty-nine inches long, extreme length forty-five inches.
Scabbard—steel.
Sword-Knot—crimson leather strap, with gold embroidered stripe; gold and crimson tassel.
Sword-Belt—gold lace two inches wide, gilt regimental front plate, two slings of gold lace, an inch wide, attached to the belt by gilt rings. The belt and slings lined with red morocco leather.
Pouch-Belt—crimson and gold, with gilt mountings, and red silk cord down centre.
Pouch-Box—black patent leather, with gilt royal arms.
Gloves—white patent leather gauntlets.
Cuirass—back and front of polished steel, with brass studs, bound with brass half an inch wide, lined throughout with red Morocco leather, and red velvet edging; scales brass, with steel studs, lined with red Morocco leather, lion's head of German silver at the ends; straps, buff leather, (with brass buckle,) one inch wide.
Trousers—dark blue, with a stripe of gold lace two inches and a quarter wide down the outward seam.

Boots—ankle.
Spurs—gilt, crane neck.

UNDRESS.

Frock-Coat—blue cloth, single breasted, with braided edges; with six braided loops and four rows of olivets down the front, stand-up collar rounded in front, ornamented with small braiding; a braiding on sleeve extending thirteen inches, from edge of cuff, on the back seams and hips, braidings terminating with fringe at the waist, and with six fringe tassels on the skirt; hooks and eyes in front; the coat lined with black silk, with relative badges on collar for F. O.

Stable-Jacket—blue cloth with scarlet edging all round, scarlet cloth collar and cuffs, collar rounded in front; pointed cuff edged round with gold half inch oak-leaf lace; hooks and eyes in front, and a row of gilt studs; plain gold cord loop on shoulder, with a small regimental button, with relative badges on collar for F. O.

Trousers—dark blue, with a stripe of scarlet cloth, two inches and a half wide, down the outward seam.

Boots—ankle.

Spurs—steel.

Sword and Scabbard—the same as in dress.

Sword-Knot—white leather.

Sword-Belt—white patent leather, two inches wide, with regimental front plate; two sword slings an inch wide, attached to the belt by gilt rings.

Pouch-Belt—white patent leather, with gilt buckles and red silk cord down centre.

Pouch—same as dress.

Forage-Cap—blue cloth, with a scarlet band, and top welt; black patent-leather peak, embroidered in gold, seven-eighths of an inch wide.

Gloves—white leather.

Cloak—blue, with scarlet collar and lining.

REGIMENTAL STAFF.

The Adjutant and Riding-Master to wear the uniform of their rank.

Coat—tunic, the Quarter Master, Surgeon, Assistant-Surgeon, and Veterinary Surgeon, wear the same coat as other Officers, with aiguillette and shoulder-strap.

Hat—cocked; the Quarter-Master to have regimental looping, tassels and a feather; the Surgeon, Assistant-Surgeon, and Veterinary Surgeon, no feather. Appointments, and other articles of dress the same as those worn by the other Officers of the Regiment.

HORSE FURNITURE.

Shabracque—Scarlet, fifty inches long, thirty-five inches deep, round front corners and pointed hind corners, laced round with two rows of gold lace; the outer lace to be three-quarters of an inch wide, and the inner one inch wide, leaving quarter of an inch blue light between, embroidered on fore and hind corners with crowns and the scrolls " Waterloo " and " Peninsula " with laurel leaves in gold, and garter star proper.

Saddle—Brown high mounting saddle, with fans, princes metal cantle, brass nails with regimental cypher.

Girth—white linen web.

Stirrup-leathers—plain.

Stirrups—square, set flat slides.

Slides—brass.

Holsters—brown; plain.

Bridle—brass head chain with cut steel studs, two rows, finished off at each end with a shield studded to match; plain leather front, with brass shield.

Bridle Undress—plain black leather with brass whole ornamented buckles. Wide plain leather head piece and front.
Collar—plain leather head collar.
Chain—steel.
Bridoon—plain ring.
Bridle Bit—steel, with beard twisted, bent bar, brass bosses with cut steel centre, mottoed garter, and crown.
Breastplate—plain leather, with boss the same as on bit.
Crupper—turnback crupper with bosses.
Surcingle—patent leather and cross rein.
Undress shabracque—black lambskin.
Valise—blue cloth twenty-four inches, six and a half inches end, R.H.G., embroidered in gold.

DRAGOON GUARDS
AND
HEAVY DRAGOONS.

Distinctions of Rank.
DRESS.

Colonel, a crown and star,
Lieutenant-Colonel, a crown,
Major, a star,

> Collar laced all round with gold lace three-quarters of an inch wide.
> Cuff, one row of gold lace round the top, loop of gold lace six inches long.

Captain, crown and star,
Lieutenants, crown,
Cornet, star.

> Collar laced round the top with gold lace.
> Cuff, loop of gold lace six inches long.

The collar badges in silver embroidery.

UNDRESS.

Field Officer, relative badges in gold, embroidery on the collar.

Other ranks, no badges to be worn.

DRESS.

Coat—tunic, scarlet, with collar, cuffs, and edging down the front, of regimental facings, which are to be of velvet for the Officers of Dragoon Guards, *and of cloth for those of Heavy Dragoons;* single-breasted, with eight regimental buttons in front at equal distances. The collar two inches deep and rounded off in front. Round cuff ten and a half inches in circumference, with a loop of three-quarter-inch gold lace, six inches long, and one button in centre. Shoulder straps of gold cord, with a small regimental button. Waist long, with two buttons and three loops of three-quarter-inch lace on each skirt behind. The skirts lined with white, nine inches deep for an Officer of five feet nine inches, with the variation of half an inch for every inch of difference in the height of wearer. Tunic collar and cuffs edged with one-quarter-inch of same material as the facings.

Helmet*—for the seven regiments of Dragoon Guards, gilt brass, the front and back peaks ornamented with a scroll wreath; a band of the same character round the bottom and up the back of the helmet; front ornament, within a shield, a diamond cut silver star, upon which is a garter bearing the title of the regiment, and encircling the cypher V.R.; above the shield a crown, and below it a wreath of olive and oak extending upwards. A chin-strap of plain chain, lined with black leather, fastening on each side to a rose ornament. On the top of the helmet a socket for plume. For the 1st or Royal Dragoons, and the 6th or Inniskilling, a helmet of white metal of the same pattern, with gilt ornaments.

---

* The Second or Royal North British Dragoons, have permission to wear a bear-skin cap with a white hackle feather, nine inches long, thistle (gilt) on the front of cap, according to sealed pattern.

The 6th Dragoon Guards (Carabiniers) retain the helmet as above described but are in other respects dressed and equipped as Light Dragoons.

Plume—horse-hair, with rose at top, standing five inches above the top of the helmet. The several regiments distinguished, as under, by the colour of the plume.

1st.	(King's) Dragoon Guards		Red.
2d.	(or Queen's)	,,	Black.
3d.	(P. W.)	,,	Black and Red.
4th.	(R. Irish)	,,	White.
5th.	(P. C. W.)	,,	Red and White.
6th.	(Carabiniers.)	,,	Black.
7th.	(Princess Rls.)	,,	Black and White.
1st.	(Royal) Dragoons		Black.
6th.	(Inniskilling)	,,	White.

Stock—black silk.

Trousers—dark blue, with a stripe of gold lace of regimental pattern, one inch and three quarters wide, down the outward seams.

Boots—Wellington.

Spurs—brass, crane necked, two inches long.

Sword—steel-mounted, half-basket hilt, with pierced scroll-work guard; black fish-skin grip bound with silver wire; the blade slightly curved, thirty-five and a half inches long, and one inch and a quarter wide.

Scabbard—steel.

Sword-Knot—white leather strap, with gold tassel.

Sword-Belt—gold lace, with an edging of velvet, colour of regimental facing, top and bottom; two inches and a half wide, lined with morocco, and fastening in front with a regulation plate same width as belt, and three inches and a quarter long, gilt frosted ground and burnished rim, a silver V.R. in the centre, surmounted by a crown and encircled with oak-leaves; the belt to have two sword slings, to fasten with a button to rings of scabbard. The belt to be worn over the coat.

Pouch-Belt—gold lace two inches and a half wide, lining and edging to correspond with sword-belt; gilt buckle, tip and slide.

Pouch-Box—black leather; gold embroidered edging round the top; solid silver flap, seven inches and a half wide, two inches and three quarters deep; engraving round the edges; gilt raised V.R. surmounted by a crown in the centre; on each side silver staple ornaments for rings of belt.

Gloves—white leather gauntlets.

UNDRESS.

Frock-Coat—blue cloth, single-breasted, with six cord loops on breast, and three rows of olivets; stand-up collar, edged with cord and braid; cord knot on sleeve, extending from edge of cuff seven inches towards the elbow; four cord loops and olivets on back and skirts; lining, black silk.

Trousers—the same as in dress, but strapped with black patent leather or sealskin, as for men.

Forage-Cap—one of pattern deposited at Army Clothing Department—blue cloth, encircled by a gold-lace band of regimental overall lace, one inch and three quarters wide; a gold netted purl button at the top; black patent leather embroidered peak; black patent leather chin-strap. The Officers of the Scot's Greys wear a gold band with vandyked edges and thistle pattern.

Stable-Jacket—scarlet round jacket, single breasted, with plain collar and pointed cuffs of the regimental facing, the collar rounded in front; the cuffs two inches deep at the back seam, and three inches at the front seam; two small buttons at the wrist; ten small regimental buttons down the front, at equal distances. On each shoulder a plain gold cord, with a small button.

Boots—Wellington.

Spurs—steel.

Gloves—white leather.

Sword-Belt—white buffalo leather, two inches and a half wide, with gilt mountings; fastening in front with gilt metal regimental plate, three inches long and two and a quarter deep, with silver V.R., crown, and laurel; two one-inch wide sword-slings. To be worn over the coat.

Pouch-Belt—white buffalo leather two inches and a half wide, with brass buckle, tip, and slide, and two brass rings, with black patent leather loops attached to them to carry the pouch-box.

Pouch-Box—the same as in dress.

Great-Coat and Cape—blue, lined with white shalloon, same pattern as sealed for rank and file.

REGIMENTAL STAFF.

The Adjutant and Riding Master to wear the uniform of their rank.

The Paymaster, Quarter-Master, Surgeon, Assistant-Surgeon, and Veterinary-Surgeon, to wear the same uniform as the other officers, except that they wear instead of the helmet a cocked hat, with gold bullion tassels, and loop one and three-eighths inches wide, formed of four rows of gold gimp chain, with regimental button.

The Quarter-Master wears a white feather drooping five inches. The Surgeon, Assistant-Surgeon, and Veterinary-Surgeon wear a feather of black cock's tail of same pattern.

The Surgeon and Assistant-Surgeon to wear also a black morocco shoulder-belt, with a small case for instruments according to pattern, instead of the regimental pouch and belt.

Paymasters wear no feathers.

LIGHT DRAGOONS.

Distinctions of Rank.

DRESS.

Colonel, crown and star.
Lieutenant-Colonel, crown.
Major, star.
{ Collar laced all round inside the gold cord with gold lace, three-quarters of an inch wide. Sleeve ornament of inch and a half lace, and narrow braid eleven inches deep.

Captain, crown and star.
Lieutenant, crown.
Cornet, star.
{ Collar laced round the top, inside the gold cord, with gold lace. Sleeve ornament of gold cord and narrow braid, eight inches deep for captains, seven for other ranks.

The collar badges in silver embroidery.

UNDRESS.

Field Officers, relative badges, in gold embroidery, on the collar.

Other ranks, no badges to be worn.

DRESS.

Jacket—tunic, blue, with collar and cuffs of regimental facings; single breasted; edged all round with gold cord.* On each side of the breast five gold cord loops with caps and drops, fastening with five gold-worked olivets; the top loop eight inches long, the bottom one four inches. Gold double cord on the shoulders, with a small regimental button. On the back seams a gold cord forming three eyes

---

* Of the pattern used for Staff Officers.

at the top, passing under a netted cap at the waist, below which it is doubled, and terminating in a knot at bottom of skirt. Waist long. The skirt nine inches deep for an officer of five feet nine inches, with the usual variation according to the height of the wearer, and lined with black, rounded off in front. The collar two inches deep, edged all round with gold cord, and rounded off at the ends. The cuffs pointed, ten and a half inches round, with two small regimental buttons.

Head-Dress—chaco body, covered with Paris velvet; height, front, five and a quarter inches; sides, six and three-eighths inches; back, nine and one-eighth inches, patent leather sunk top, one inch and one-eighth less in diameter than size of head; patent leather five-eighths of an inch band round bottom of cap, gold inch and three quarters oak band round top of cap; nearly horizontal patent leather three-quarters of an inch gold embroidered peak projecting two and a quarter inches; burnished gilt plain chain three-quarters of an inch wide, with rose ornaments each side of chaco, gilt lion head with ring immediately below gold band at back of chaco; also gilt hook to fasten up chain, front ornament, gilt and silver Maltese cross, with crown above according to regimental patterns deposited. Line. Gold gimp and orris cord, with sliders and olive ends, worn once single round the chaco and round the neck. Gilt plume socket corded ball, with four upright rays of following colours, for—

3 L. D. black and white,
4 L. D. scarlet,
13 L. D. white,
14 L. D. red and white.

Hair plume standing five inches above top of chaco.

Stock—black silk.

Trousers—dark blue, with two stripes down each outward seam, of gold lace, three quarters of an inch wide, leaving a light between.

Boots—Wellington.

Spurs—yellow metal, crane necked, two inches long.

Sword—steel-mounted, half-basket hilt, with two fluted bars on the outside, black fish-skin gripe bound with silver wire; the blade slightly curved, thirty-five inches and a half long, and one inch and a quarter wide, with a round back, terminating within eleven inches of the point.

Scabbard—steel, with large shoe at the bottom, solid band and rings, a trumpet-formed mouth.

Sword-Knot—gold cord, with acorn end.

Sword-Belt—gold lace one inch and a quarter wide, with a quarter-inch silk stripe up the centre; morocco lining and edging, fastened in front with a snake ornament; two gilt rings, through which hang two slings of one inch and a quarter wide gold and silk lace, to fasten with a button to rings of scabbard; the silk stripes, and morocco lining and edging, of the colour of facings. The belt to be worn under the jacket.

Pouch-Belt—gold lace, two inches wide, with half-inch silk stripe, lining, and edging, to correspond with waist-belt; silver engraved plates with chains and pickers, buckle, tip, and slide; attached to pouch-box with silver buckles and rings.

Pouch-Box—black leather, a gold embroidered edging round the top; solid silver flap, seven inches and a half wide, two inches and three-quarters deep; engraving round the edges; gilt raised V.R., surmounted by a crown, in the centre; on each side silver staple ornaments for rings of belt.

Gloves—white leather.

UNDRESS.

Frock-Coat—same as for Heavy Dragoons. Pattern deposited at Army Clothing Department.

Trousers—blue, with two stripes down each outward seam,

of pale yellow cloth, three-quarters of an inch wide, leaving a light between,* strapped with patent leather as for men.

Forage-Cap—blue cloth, with welts and plaits; band one inch and three-quarters wide of lace, same pattern as worn on trousers, a figure in gold Russia braid on top; black patent leather peak, embroidered, chin-strap, and oil-skin cover, according to sealed pattern at Army Clothing Department.

Stable-Jacket—blue round jacket, single-breasted, with plain collar and pointed cuffs of the regimental facing; the collar rounded in front; the cuffs two inches deep at the back seam, and three inches at the front seam; two small buttons at the wrist; ten small regimental buttons down the front at equal distances; on each shoulder a plain gold cord with a small button. Field Officers to wear distinctive badge on the collar.

Spurs—steel, crane necked, with sharp rowels, two inches long.

Gloves—white leather.

Sword-Belt—black patent leather, two inches wide, with gilt lion's head mounting, fastening in front with a snake-ornament; two gilt rings, through which hang two sword-slings, each one inch wide, to fasten with a button to rings of scabbard. The belt to be worn under the jacket.

Pouch-Belt—plain white buffalo leather, two inches wide, attached to pouch-box.

Pouch-Box—same as dress.

Great-Coat and Cape—blue cloth, lined with scarlet. Same pattern as that sealed for rank and file.

DRESS OF REGIMENTAL STAFF.

The Adjutant and Riding Master to wear the uniform of their rank.

The Dress and Undress of the other Officers of the Regimental Staff are to be the same as those worn by the rest of the Officers, except that their head-dress, shoulder belt, &c., are to be the same as prescribed for Heavy Cavalry, page 84.

---

* In the 13th Light Dragoons the stripes are buff, according to the regimental facings.

HUSSARS.

Distinctions of Rank.

DRESS.

Colonel, crown and star,
Lieut.-Colonel, crown,
Major, star.
{ Collars laced all round with gold lace, three-quarters of an inch wide, a figured braiding within the lace. Sleeve ornament, knot of gold chain lace, with figured braiding eight inches deep.

Captain, crown and star.
{ Collar laced round the top with gold lace, and a figured braiding. Sleeve ornament, knot of gold chain lace, and figured braiding eight inches deep.

Lieutenant, crown.
Cornet, star.
{ Collar laced round the top with gold lace, with a plain edging of gold braid within the lace. Sleeve ornament, knot of gold chain lace, edged with braid seven inches deep.

The collar badges in silver embroidery.

UNDRESS.

Field Officers, relative badges in gold embroidery on collar.
Other ranks, no badges to be worn.

DRESS.

Jacket—tunic, entirely of blue cloth; single-breasted; the collar two inches high, rounded in front. On each side of the breast, six loops of gold chain lace, with caps and drops, fastening with six gold worked olivets; the top loop eight inches long, the bottom one four inches. The jacket edged all round (except the collar) with gold chain lace. On the back seams a double chain of the same lace, edged with braid forming three eyes at top, passing under a netted cap at the waist, and terminating in a knot at bottom of skirt. Waist long; the skirt nine inches deep for an Officer of five feet nine inches in height, with the variation before described, and lined with black. Cuffs ten and a half inches round.

Waistcoat—scarlet, with half-ball buttons, and ornamented with gold cord. (Not worn in the 8th or 11th Hussars.)

Cap, Busby—black sable fur, falling half an inch all round below the body or framework of the cap. Outside measurement, front seven and three quarters inches; sides eight inches; back nine inches; top nine-sixteenths less than bottom; front half-inch out of perpendicular; back, capped to fit the head; a gold gimp oval cockade, two inches long, one and a half inches broad in centre of front, fixed on a level with the top edge of cap, gilt ring for line fixed at top of right side of cap underneath the fly; gilt hook at top of right side to loop up chain; spring socket in centre of front for plume; fly or bag, crimson cloth for 11th Hussars, scarlet cloth for other regiments, seam in front covered with a single line of gold figuring braid, and a single line of gold figuring braid down the centre. At the point of junction a gold gimp one-inch button.

Cap-Chain—dead and bright gilt corded, fixed to left side by an eye or loop, and attachable to right side by a hook.

Cap Line—gold pearl cord, with sliders and olive ends to match, encircling the cap diagonally three times, and worn round the neck.

Plume—eight inches high above top of cap, encircled by a gold ring.

7th Regiment, entire white osprey feathers.
8th   „   the same, but lower third covered with red feathers.
10th „   the same, but lower third covered with black feathers.
11th „   the same, but lower third covered with crimson feathers.
15th „   entire scarlet osprey feathers.

Plume-Socket—gilt corded ball, with four upright leaves.
Stock—black silk.
Trousers—dress, blue cloth, stripe of gold regimental lace, one inch and a half wide down outer seam.
Boots—Wellington.
Spurs—yellow metal, crane neck, two inches long.
Sword—same as Light Dragoons.
Scabbard—idem.
Sword-Knot—gold and crimson, with a large acorn.
Sword-Belt—gold lace, one inch and a quarter wide, with scarlet morocco edging and lining, fastened in front with a clasp ornament; gilt mountings, and three rings, from which hang two sword-slings of similar width, with loops and buckles for rings of scabbard, and three half-inch tache-slings, with loops and buckles for rings of tache. The belt to be worn under the jacket.
Sabretache—scarlet cloth* face, laced with gold lace, two inches and a quarter wide, leaving an edge of scarlet; embroidered regimental badge in the centre, three gilt rings at top; pocket, scarlet morocco; slings short enough to prevent sabre-tache from hanging below the calf of the leg.
Pouch-Belt—gold lace, one inch a half wide, scarlet cloth edging, and morocco lining; gilt ornamented buckle, tip, and slide; attached to sides of pouch.†
Pouch-Box—scarlet cloth; circular flap, five inches deep, six inches wide at top, six and a half at bottom, edged round with gold braid and embroidery; embroidered regimental badge in centre.
Gloves—white leather.

---

* In the 11th Hussars, the cloth face and morocco pocket of the sabretache, and the lining and edging of the belts, are crimson instead of scarlet; and a pouch-box is sanctioned, of gilt metal with silver ornaments, according to regimental pattern.

† The 10th Hussars are permitted to wear, both in dress and undress, a pouch and pouch-belt, of black patent leather, according to regimental patterns.

UNDRESS.

Frock-Coat—blue cloth, single-breasted, with six flat braided loops, and four rows of olivets on breast; stand-up collar, edged with flat braid, and with figuring inside; sleeves, braid extending from edge of cuff ten inches towards the elbow; back and skirt, braided with broad and narrow braid, and with olivets and tassels, lined with black silk and with relative collar badge for Field Officers. Sealed pattern at Army Clothing Department.

Trousers—blue cloth, with a pale yellow stripe, one inch and a half wide, down the outward seam; and strapped with patent leather, as before directed.

Forage-Cap—blue cloth; a gold band of regimental lace, same as worn on trousers, one inch and three quarters wide, a gold braided ornament and purl button at top; the seam of the crown of the cap encircled with gold braid; without peak, oil-skin cover.*

Stable-Jacket—blue; single breasted, with olivets and gold lace according to regimental pattern and relative collar badge for F. O.

Spurs—steel, crane neck, two inches long.

Sword-Knot—of regimental pattern.

Sabretache
Belt†
Pouch
Pouch-Belt
} black patent leather, with gilt mountings.

Great-Coat and Cape—blue cloth, lined with scarlet (except in the 8th Regiment, where the lining is white, and in the 11th, where it is crimson); same pattern as for Heavy Dragoons, page 84.

REGIMENTAL STAFF.

The Adjutant and Riding Master to wear the uniform of their rank.

---

* The forage-cap in the 11th Hussars is of crimson cloth, and in the 15th of scarlet.

† In the 10th and 11th Regiments, Russia leather.

LANCERS. 93

The Dress and Undress of the other Officers of the Regimental staff, as before directed for Heavy Cavalry, page 84.

LANCERS.

Distinctions of Rank.

DRESS.

Colonel, crown and star.
Lieutenant-Colonel, crown,
Major, star.
{ Collar laced all round with gold lace, one inch wide. Cuff pointed with two rows of lace, showing a light between the rows.

Captain, crown and star,
Lieutenant, crown,
Cornet, star.
{ Collar laced round the top with gold lace, one inch wide. Cuff pointed with one row of lace.

The collar badges in silver embroidery.

UNDRESS.

Field Officers, relative badges in gold embroidery on the collar. *Other ranks*, no badges to be worn.

DRESS.

Jacket—tunic, blue; double-breasted, two rows of buttons seven in each row (the bottom one flat, to go under the girdle), the distance between the rows eight inches at top, four at bottom. Lappels of regimental facings to be worn buttoned back, excepting on the line of march or in bad weather; skirts nine inches deep, for an officer of five feet nine inches in height, and with the usual variation, and lined with black. Collar two inches deep, of regimental facing, and rounded in front, with distinctions of rank, as stated above. Waist long; plain pointed cuff, ten and a half inches round, of regimental facing, with two small regimental buttons. On each shoulder a double gold cord, with a small regimental button. Two regimental buttons at the hips; blue slash on each skirt, with three regimental buttons, and edged with gold cord. A welt of the regimental facings in the sleeve and back seams, down the edge of the front and round the skirts.*

Stock—black silk.

Trousers—blue cloth, with two stripes down each outward seam, of gold lace, three quarters of an inch wide, leaving a light between.

Boots—Wellington.

Spurs—yellow metal, two inches long, with dumb rowels; crane necked.

Sword—as for Light Dragoons.

Scabbard—idem.

Sword-Knot—gold and crimson cord strap, with acorn.

Girdle—gold lace, two and a half inches wide, with two crimson silk stripes.

Sword-Belt—gold lace, one and a quarter inch wide, with quarter-inch silk stripe up centre; morocco lining and edging, fastening in front with a snake ornament; two gilt rings, from which hang two one inch and a quarter gold and silk lace slings for sabre, fastening with gilt buckles and leather straps; the silk stripes, and morocco lining and edging, to be of the colour of the regimental facing. The belt to be worn under the jacket.

Pouch-Belt—gold lace, two inches wide, with half-inch silk stripe, morocco lining and edging, to correspond with waist-belt; silver plate with pickers and chains, buckle, tip, and slide.

Pouch-Box—scarlet leather; a gold embroidered edging round the top; solid silver flap, seven inches and a half wide, two and three quarters deep, ornamented with gilt raised solid V.R. and crown; attached to belt by staples and rings.†

Gloves—white leather gauntlets.

---

* The 16th Lancers wear a scarlet jacket, with blue facings and welts.

† The pouch-box of the 9th and 17th Lancers is blue leather instead of scarlet, and that of the 9th has the double cypher A.R.

NINTH LANCERS.

Cap—skull and top covered with black patent leather, the upper part only covered with blue cloth; dimensions of cap same as other Lancer regiments; gilt metal ornaments at four corners of top attached to gilt metal strips covering the angles; on left side a gilt metal rosette with regimental screw and button in centre, and at back of rosette a socket for plume stem. A gilt metal one inch band round waist, at back a ring and hook for line and chain. A gilt plate with double A. R. cypher and gilt arms to match, with badges according to regimental pattern as deposited. Black patent leather peak with gilt metal quarter inch binding, gilt corded chain five-eighths of an inch, attached to lions' heads at side of cap.

Line and Plume-Socket—as in other Lancer regiments.

Plume—black and white cocktail feathers, size as in other Lancer regiments.

TWELFTH, SIXTEENTH, AND SEVENTEENTH LANCERS.

Cap—skull covered with black patent leather, the upper part and top with cloth same colour as facings; height in front six and a half inches, side seven inches, back eight and a half inches, top, seven and a quarter inches square. Gold gimp and orris cord across the top and down the angles; on left side a gold bullion rosette with embroidered V.R. on blue velvet for 12th and 17th Lancers and scarlet for 16th Lancers, at the back of which a socket for plume stem. A band of gold one inch lace round the waist, with two bands of gold braid below, the upper half inch wide the lower quarter inch wide, a space of one-eighth of an inch being left between the lace and the two braids; a similar double band of braid round the bottom of the skull; the half inch braid at the bottom and the quarter of an inch above it with a space of an eighth of an inch between. A gilt plate with silver arms and badge, according to regimental pattern as deposited. Black patent leather peak embroidered with three rows of gold purl, in all one inch and a quarter wide. Plain gilt burnished five-eighths of an inch chain attached to lions' heads at side of cap. Gilt rings and hook at back of waist for line and chain.

Line—Gold gimp and orris cord with slide and olive ends passing through ring at back and encircling the cap singly and worn round the neck.

Plume—cocktail feathers, twelve inches long and standing four and a half inches above top of cap.

Colour for— 12th lancers, scarlet,
     16th ,, scarlet and white,
     17th ,, white.

Gilt plume socket corded ball with four upright rays.

UNDRESS.

Frock-Coat—same as for Heavy and Light Dragoons, with relative collar badge for F. O.

Trousers—blue cloth, with two pale yellow* stripes, three-quarters of an inch wide, down each outward seam, showing a light between. Strapped as before directed.

Forage-Cap—blue cloth; a gold band of regimental lace, same as worn on trousers, one inch and three quarters wide; a gold netted purl button at top, with gold braid crossing the top of the cap twice, and terminating under the lace band; gold embroidered peak, oil-skin cover.

Stable-Jacket—blue round jacket, single-breasted, with plain collar, pointed cuffs, and welts in the sleeve and back seams, of the regimental facing; the collar rounded in front; the cuffs four inches and a half at the point, rounded off to an inch and three-quarters; two small

---

* In the 17th Lancers the stripes are white, the colour of the regimental facings.

buttons at wrist; ten small regimental buttons down the front, at equal distances. On each shoulder a plain gold cord with small button. Field Officers to wear distinctive badge on the collar.

Spurs—steel; two inches long, including sharp rowels, crane neck.

Sword-Belt—in the 9th Lancers, brown morocco leather, with regimental ornaments; in the 16th, black patent leather; in the 12th and 17th, *as in dress*.

Gloves—white leather.

Great-Coat and Cape—as for Light Dragoons, page 88.

REGIMENTAL STAFF.

The Adjutant and Riding Master to wear the uniform of their rank.

The Dress and Undress of the other officers of the Regimental Staff as before directed, page 84.

HORSE FURNITURE
OR
CAVALRY OFFICERS

OF ALL REGIMENTS EXCEPTING THE HOUSEHOLD BRIGADE.

Saddle—Hussar brown-hogskin, brass head and cantle; Hussar stirrup-leathers and irons, blue girths.

Bridle—brown leather, with brass wire whole buckles, bent branch bit, with pads, and plain bent bar link and tee bridoon; plain leather head collar, bit-head, and bridoon rein sewn on; regimental bosses on bit, and face piece. Hussar regiments to have hair throat ornaments, of regimental colours, as in shaco, 18 inches in length, with brass ball and socket.

Chain—steel.

G

Breastplate—brown leather, with brass wire, whole buckles, and regimental boss, on stitched leather heart.

Crupper—brown leather single strap, with regimental boss, and buckles as before.

Surcingle and Shabracque strap—brown leather.

Dress Lambskin—black Ukraine lambskin, three feet four inches long, thirteen and a half inches in depth, lined moleskin, trimmed scarlet cloth.

Undress Lambskin—black Ukraine lambskin with leather seat, and large flap to open for wallets, lined moleskin, trimmed scarlet cloth. *

NOTE.—The 7th and 10th Hussars are permitted to wear the leopard skins, in lieu of the lambskin. Sealed patterns thereof deposited at Army Clothing Department.

Valise—red cloth for heavy, and blue for light, cavalry, twenty-seven inches long, hollowed to centre, ends six and a half inches in diameter, embroidered with Arabic number and relative regimental initial letters.

NOTE.—The numbers on all military equipments to be as directed by Queen's regulations, in the Arabic character.

Sealed patterns of the regimental bosses are deposited at the Army Clothing Board.

SHABRACQUES.

(OF WHICH SEALED PATTERNS ARE DEPOSITED AT THE ARMY CLOTHING DEPARTMENT.)

HEAVY CAVALRY.

To be of blue cloth, cut square, three feet three inches in length, two feet two inches in depth, trimmed with gold overall lace, lined moleskin.

---

* White cloth edging to dress and undress lambskin of 17th Lancers, and buff cloth for 13th Light Dragoons.

LIGHT DRAGOONS AND LANCER REGIMENTS.

To be of blue cloth, cut round before and behind, three feet eleven inches in length, two feet six inches in depth, trimmed with gold overall lace, lined moleskin.

HUSSAR REGIMENTS.

To be of blue cloth, cut with a peak behind, and squared off in front, four feet four inches in length, three feet one inch in depth, trimmed gold overall lace, lined moleskin.

THE DEVICES FOR THE TWENTY-THREE REGIMENTS OF CAVALRY.

1st, or KING'S DRAGOON GUARDS.

To have on fore corners, V.R. and crown in gold; on hind corners, crown, V.R. within garter, with Royal Motto round it, and 1. D.G. under, all gold.

2nd DRAGOON GUARDS.

To have on fore corners, V.R. and crown in gold; on hind corners, crown over V.R. within garter, with the words (The Queen's Bays) round it, and 2 D.G. under, all gold.

3rd DRAGOON GUARDS.

To have on fore corners, V.R. and crown in gold; on hind corners, crown over plume, with coronet and scroll (Ich Dien), and 3 D.G. under; the plume to be silver, and the rest gold.

4th DRAGOON GUARDS.

To have on fore corners, V.R. and crown in gold; on hind corners, crown over harp and 4 D.G. under it The harp-strings silver, and the rest gold.

5th DRAGOON GUARDS.

To have on fore corners, V.R. and crown in gold; on hind corners, crown over 5, within garter, with motto (Vestigia nulla retrorsum) round it, and D.G. under, all gold.

6th DRAGOON GUARDS.

To have on fore corners, V.R. and crown in gold; on hind corners, crown over crossed carbines, then scroll with the word (Carabineers) and 6 D.G. under, all gold.

7th DRAGOON GUARDS.

To have on fore corners, V.R. and crown in gold; on hind corners, crown over garter, with the words (Princess Royal's) round it, and 7 D.G. within the garter, all gold.

1st DRAGOONS.

To have on fore corners, V.R. and crown in gold; on hind corners, crown over Royal Crest within garter, with the motto (Spectemur agendo) round it, and 1 D. under, all gold.

2nd DRAGOONS.

To have on fore corners, V.R. and crown in gold; on hind corners, crown over thistle within garter, with the motto (Nemo me impune lacessit) round it, then the scroll (second to none) and 2 D. under. The thistle silver, the rest gold.

3rd LIGHT DRAGOONS.

To have on fore corners, V.R. and crown in gold; on hind corners, crown over, horse on scarlet, with green hill within garter, with the motto (Nec aspera terrent) round it, and 3 L.D. under it. Horse silver, the rest gold.

4th LIGHT DRAGOONS.

To have on fore corners, V.R. and crown in gold; on hind corners, crown over, $\mathcal{D}$ in cypher, and 4 L.D. under it, all gold. A light of scarlet cloth, quarter inch, between the laces.

6th DRAGOONS.

To have on fore corners, V.R. and crown in gold; on hind corners, crown over scroll (Inniskilling), then castle and 6 D. under it. The castle silver embroidered, with the green hills, and the rest gold.

7th HUSSARS.

To have on fore corners, V.R. and crown in gold; on hind corners, crown over V.R., within garter, with the words (The Queen's Own) round it, and 7 H. under it, all gold.

8th HUSSARS.

To have on fore corners, V.R. and crown in gold; on hind corners, crown over harp, then scroll with motto (Pristinæ Virtutis Memores) with 8 H. under it, all gold, except harp strings, silver.

9th LANCERS.

To have on fore corners, V.R. and crown in gold, on hind corners, crown over V.R., within garter, with the words (Ninth Lancers) round it, and the lances crossed under the garter, all gold.

10th HUSSARS.

To have on fore corners, V.R. and crown in gold, on hind corners, crown over plume, with coronet and (Ich Dien) within scroll (Prince of Wales's Own), enclosing 10 and H. under it, plume in silver, the rest in gold.

11th HUSSARS.

To have on fore corners, V.R. and crown in gold; on hind corners, crown over sphynx, then scroll (Prince Albert's Own Hussars), enclosing 11 and H. under it. Sphynx silver embroidery, the rest in gold.

The two rows of regimental lace, on crimson cloth quarter inch apart, and showing likewise quarter-inch of crimson beyond the outer edges;

12th LANCERS.

To have on fore corners, V.R. and crown in gold; on hind corners, crowns over plume on crossed lances; then sphynx and 12 L. under it; plume and sphynx silver embroidery, the rest gold.

13th LIGHT DRAGOONS.

To have on fore corners V.R. and crown in gold; on hind corners, crown over 13, within garter, surrounded with the motto (*Viret in Æternum*), and L. D. under it, all gold.

14th LIGHT DRAGOONS.

To have on fore corners V.R. and crown in gold; on hind corners, crown over V.R., in garter, with (14th Light Dragoons) round it, and Prussian eagle under it, all gold.

15th HUSSARS.

To have on fore corners, V.R. and crown in gold; on hind corners, crown over Queen's crest, within garter, with the word (M erebimur) round it; then the crossed flags reversed, and 15 H. under it; flags in silver, the rest gold embroidery.

16th LANCERS.

To have on fore corners V.R. and crown in gold; on hind corners, crown over V.R. within garter, on crossed lances, and 16 L. under it; all gold.

17th LANCERS.

To have on fore corners, V.R. and crown in gold; on hind corners, crown over scull and cross bones on crossed lances, with the scrolls bearing the motto "Or Glory," and 17 L. under it; scull and crossed bones silver metal, the rest gold.

MILITARY TRAIN.

Distinctions of Rank.

DRESS.

Col. Commandant—Uniform of a Field Officer of the corps, with cocked hat and plume as for Staff Officers, page 16. and horse furniture as at page 30.

Col.—crown and star.
Lt. Col.—crown.
Major—star.
{ Collar laced all round with gold lace inside the gold cord. Sleeve ornament of inch lace and figured braiding eleven inches deep.

Captain—crown and star. Collar laced round the top with gold lace inside the gold cord.

Sleeve ornament, knot of gold cord and figured braiding, eight inches deep.

Lieut.—crown.
Cornet—star.
{ Collar laced round the top with gold lace inside the gold cord. Sleeve ornament, knot of gold cord edged with braid seven inches deep.

The collar badges in silver embroidery.

UNDRESS.

Field Officers—relative badges in gold embroidery on collar.
Other ranks—no badges to be worn.

DRESS.

Coat—tunic; blue, with white collar, single breasted, and edged all round with white, one-quarter inch wide; blue double cord on the shoulders; eight holes, and buttons down the front at equal distances. The skirt nine inches deep for an officer of five feet nine inches in height, with usual variation, and lined with black, the collar two inches deep and edged all round with gold cord, and rounded off at the ends. Blue cuffs, pointed ten and a-half inches round, with two small regimental buttons.

Head-Dress—chaco; black beaver, Light Cavalry pattern black, inch and five-eighths mohair oak-leaf band round top. Peak of plain patent leather; leather chin strap five-eighths inch wide, fastening inside cap; the plate a double gilt oak branch enclosing a garter with the words "Military Train" on black, and the number of the battalion inserted inside the garter. Bronzed Gorgon's head ventilator at back; gilt plume-socket, of light dragoon pattern, and a black horse-hair plume. Black cap line, with barrels and egg ends.

Stock—black silk.

Trousers—dark blue, with one stripe of gold lace, staff pattern, one inch wide, on white cloth.

Boots—Wellington.

Spurs—yellow metal, crane neck.

Sword—steel; mounted as Light Cavalry steel scabbard.

Sword Knot—gold cord with acorn end.

Sword-Belt—pale Russia leather, one inch and a-half wide, with two rows gold straight embroidery. Slings embroidered on one side, plain; gilt buckles to slings; plate gilt, with gilt M. T. and number of battalion beneath.

Pouch-Belt—pale Russia leather, two inches and a quarter wide, with two rows gold embroidery, waved; gilt buckle, tip, and slide.

Pouch-Box—pale Russia leather, with two rows gold embroidery round; gilt leaf, ends gilt; M. T. on flap, and number of battalion beneath.

STAFF OFFICERS OF MILITARY TRAIN.

The Brigade Major, Military Train, to wear the uniform as directed for Brigade Majors, page 30, except that the tunic is to be of blue cloth, with the white facings of the corps. The gold lace of dress trousers to be on white cloth, and the undress trousers to be same as for officers of the corps, but strapped with leather as for cavalry. Horse Furniture as directed, page 30.

The paymasters, quartermasters, surgeons, and assistant-surgeons to wear the same uniform as the other officers, except that instead of the chaco they wear a cocked hat, with gold double lace, loop, bullion tassels, and regimental button.

The quartermaster to wear a *white* cock tail plume.

The surgeon and assistant-surgeon and veterinary-surgeon, a black cock tail plume.

The paymaster no plume.

The surgeons and assistant-surgeons to wear in lieu of the brown belts, a black Morocco sling belt, with plate, and also a black Morocco shoulder belt, with a small case for instruments.

UNDRESS OF OFFICERS OF MILITARY TRAIN.

Frock-Coat—blue, single breasted, rolling collar, with five loops, three-quarter inch mohair braid on each side, two rows olivets, pointed cuff, with three quarters inch mohair braid, and trimmed to regimental pattern; on the skirts three streamers of three quarters inch mohair braid, with tassels, with relative collar badge for Field Officers.

Waistcoat—plain blue cloth, single breasted, without collar, fastening down the front with hook eyes. To be worn with blue frock coat.

Forage-Cap, of infantry form—blue cloth with mohair oak leaf band, and black braided top, plain peak, and regimental badge.

Stable Jacket—blue; single breasted, white collar, blue pointed cuffs, four inches and a half deep, two small buttons at the wrist, ten small buttons down front, at equal distances; the jacket and cuffs edged completely round with white kerseymere, one quarter inch wide on each shoulder, a double blue cord with small button. Field Officers to wear relative badges on collar.

Trousers—blue; with one inch and a half white stripe.

Sword-Belt—plain, brown leather, with slings and gilt snake front.

Pouch-Belt—plain brown leather.

Pouch—plain brown leather, with gilt M. T. and battalion number on flap.

Cloak—cavalry shape, infantry colour.

Horse Furniture—of the several grades of Officers in the military train to correspond with those of similar rank in Royal Artillery, with the substitution of white for red cloth according to the respective facings, with lace of the corps. The Field and Staff Officers provide their own horse furniture; that for the Troop Officers is provided by Army Clothing Department, of the same pattern as that for Officers of the Batteries, Royal Artillery, except that the sheepskin has an edging of white instead of red cloth.

DRESS OF OFFICERS

OF

REGIMENTS OF INFANTRY.

FOOT GUARDS.

INFANTRY OF THE LINE.

LIGHT INFANTRY.

FUSILIERS.

HIGHLAND REGIMENTS.

RIFLE REGIMENTS.

HORSE FURNITURE FOR MOUNTED OFFICERS OF INFANTRY.

CAPE MOUNTED RIFLES.

WEST INDIA REGIMENTS.

ROYAL NEWFOUNDLAND COMPANIES.

ROYAL MALTA FENCIBLES.

SCHOOL OF MUSKETRY.

GOLD COAST CORPS ARTILLERY.

UNATTACHED OFFICERS, AND OFFICERS ON HALF-PAY.

OFFICERS WHO HAVE RETIRED ON FULL PAY.

OFFICERS WHO HAVE LEFT THE ARMY, BUT WHOSE NAMES ARE ALLOWED TO REMAIN IN THE ARMY LIST.

ROYAL ARTILLERY.

ROYAL ENGINEERS.

BARRACK MASTERS.

CIVIL DEPARTMENT OF THE WAR OFFICE.

OFFICERS
OF
REGIMENTS OF INFANTRY.

The blue frock-coat, according to regulation, with the waist-belt and sword, and the sash over the left shoulder, is to be worn in quarters, on fatigue or orderly duties, at drill, and on parade, when the non-commissioned officers and men are dressed in shell jackets.

The sash over the left shoulder and the white waist-belt and sword are to be worn on all occasions, both with the scarlet coat and the blue frock. The forage cap is to be worn with the blue frock, never with the scarlet coat.

When regimental Officers attend in uniform, as spectators, the review or inspection of troops by the Commander-in-Chief, or by any General Officer, they are to appear in the uniform of their respective regiments, and not in the blue frock-coat.

Officers in mourning, when dressed in uniform, are to wear a piece of black crape round the left arm above the elbow.

At Court, and on all occasions when Officers appear in the scarlet coat, they are to wear the waist-belt and the sash over the left shoulder, the ends of the fringe not to hang below the bottom of the coat.

The *Shell Jacket* may be worn at mess and on those occasions when the blue frock is worn at home, by regiments serving at the under-mentioned stations, viz. :—

East Indies.	Mediterranean.
China.	West Indies and Jamaica.
Ceylon.	Canada.
Mauritius.	West Coast of Africa.
Cape of Good Hope.	New South Wales.
Gibraltar.	

Officers who have retired from the service and are permitted to retain their rank in the army, or who may be Companions of the Bath, may appear in the unattached uniform when attending Her Majesty's levees or drawing-rooms.

Brevet Field Officers, doing duty with their regiments as captains, to wear the distinctive badges and lace on their coats according to their rank in the army, with the leather scabbard upon all duties on foot. When required to perform mounted duties, they will be permitted to wear, on those occasions, the brass scabbard and spurs.

The dress and appointments of the Officers of Militia are in every respect conformable to the patterns established for the line, with the following exceptions:—

Silver is in all cases substituted for gold; the crowns and stars, as badges of rank, are to be embroidered in gold upon the scarlet uniform, and in silver upon the blue frock-coat, and the cap-plates are according to a pattern deposited at the Army Clothing Department. When Officers of the Militia are permitted to serve upon the Staff, they are to wear the uniform of their regiment.

FOOT GUARDS.

Coat—tunic, scarlet, single-breasted, with collar and cuffs of blue cloth, buttons as directed below down the front, and a fly one and three-quarters inch wide, thus buttoning well over; the waist long; the collar two inches high and rounded off in front, the fronts of the collar embroidered in gold, with the badge of the regiment raised in silver embroidery on the gold. The cuff ten and a half inches round, and two and three-quarters inches deep; the slashed flap on sleeve blue, five and a half inches long and two and a quarter inches broad, embroidered in gold.

FOOT GUARDS.

The Grenadier Regiment is to have a silver grenade at each end of the collar. The buttons (nine in number) on the front are to be placed at equal distances; four bars of embroidery on the skirt and sleeve flaps, also at equal distances.

The Coldstream Regiment is to have the star of the order of the garter on the collar. The buttons are to be ten in number, and placed two and two, and the bars of embroidery on the skirt and sleeve flaps also two and two.

The Scots Fusilier Regiment is to have the thistle on the collar. The buttons (nine in number) are to be placed three and three; three buttons and bars of embroidery on the skirt flaps and sleeve flaps, and two hip buttons.

The skirt of the coat to be $10\frac{1}{2}$ inches deep for an Officer five feet nine inches in height, with a variation of half an inch longer or shorter for every inch of difference in the height of the wearer. The hip buttons to stand three inches apart; scarlet flaps at the plaits ten and a half inches long. On the left shoulder a scarlet silk cord and regimental button to retain the sash.

The coat, collar, cuffs, and flaps edged with white one quarter of an inch wide, and the skirts lined with white.

The Field Officers and Captains to be distinguished by embroidery round the top and bottom of the collar, also on the edge of the skirt flaps, and edge of sleeve flaps; two rows of embroidery round the top of the cuffs, and the following badges embroidered in silver at each end of the collar, viz. :—

Field Officers and Colonels, a crown and star.

Captains, a crown.

Lieutenants who are Brevet-Majors, a star.

The other Officers are to have embroidery on the top only of the collar, and one row round the cuffs; none round the skirt flaps or sleeve flaps, and the following badges at each end of the collar, viz. :—

Lieutenants, a crown and star.

Ensigns, a crown.

The embroidery to be half an inch in width.

Buttons to be of a uniform size, of the sealed pattern, with the regimental devices, except on the shoulder, where it is to be small.

Cap—bearskin, eight inches deep, fastened under the chin by a plain gilt taper chain.

Plume—for the Grenadier Regiment, white goat's hair, six inches long, worn on the left side; for the Coldstream Regiment, scarlet cut feather, six inches long, worn on the right side; the Scots Fusilier Regiment wear no plume.

Stock—black silk.

Trousers—blue cloth, with a stripe of gold lace, one inch and a half wide, down each outward seam, for levees, drawing-rooms, and in the evening. On other occasions, from the 15th of October to the 30th of April, Oxford mixture, with a stripe of scarlet cloth, one inch and a half wide down the outward seam; from the 1st of May to the 14th of October, grey, of same pattern, only of lighter texture, with same stripes.

Sword—steel-mounted, half-basket hilt, with the distinctive badge of each Regiment pierced and chased in the guard, viz. :—

    1st Grenadiers, the grenade and V.R.
    2nd Coldstream, star and motto.
    3rd Fusiliers, star and motto.

The blade same dimensions as that for Officers of the Line (see page 118), and embossed with battles and devices to the Regimental pattern.

Scabbard of steel, lined with wood, and with German silver mouth-piece.

Sword-Knot—gold acorn and gold twisted cord in full dress; on other occasions, gilt acorn, white twisted cord.

Sword-Belt—for dress occasions, of inch-and-a-half gold lace, with carriages of inch lace. For ordinary use, of enamelled white leather, the same width, with slings and a gilt hook. The belt to be worn over the coat.

Plate—a round clasp, gilt, with the regimental badge on the centre piece, and the title of the regiment on the outer circle.

Sash—crimson and gold on state occasions; at other times, crimson silk patent net. To be worn over the shoulder, and the ends of the fringe not to hang below the bottom of the coat.

Boots—Wellington.

Spurs—for mounted Officers, yellow metal crane necks, two inches long.

Gloves—white leather.

Frock-Coat—blue cloth, braided, according to regimental pattern, and with relative collar badge for the regimental F. Officers, and worn with white sword-belt.

Forage-Cap—blue cloth, with band, one inch and a half wide; leather peak, with embroidery half an inch wide; and chin-strap. For Grenadier Guards, black braid band and embroidered grenade in front; for Coldstream Guards, black braid band and embroidered star of the garter; for Scots Fusilier Guards, royal tartan band, gold cord round the edge of the crown, and Saint Andrew's star in front.

Great Coat—grey, of the regimental pattern.

REGIMENTAL STAFF.

The Adjutant to wear the uniform of his rank.

Medical Officers

to wear the Regimental Uniform of their respective ranks, with the exception of the bearskin cap, sash, and sword-belt. The distinctions of a Surgeon-Major to be the same as for

Captains. For Battalion-Surgeons and Assistant-Surgeons the same as for Lieutenants and Ensigns.

Hat—cocked, bound with two inch black silk binding; fan or back part, nine inches; front, seven inches and a half; each corner, five inches; gold lace regimental loop and button, tassels composed of gold crape fringe with crimson crape fringe underneath, and a feather of black cock's tail, drooping from a feathered stem three inches in length.

Sword-Belt—black, with gilt mountings, worn over the coat, of the same pattern as the belts for other Officers. The Battalion-Surgeon and Assistant-Surgeon will also wear a shoulder belt, with a small case of instruments, according to pattern.

Quarter-Master.

Coat—the same as for subaltern Officers; but no distinguishing mark on the collar.

Hat—as above described; with regimental feather, five inches long.

Sash—crimson silk net.

Belt—the same as that worn by Medical Officers.

The Solicitor

is to wear a plain blue coat, with red collar and cuff, and regimental button; cocked hat, with black loop and button. No sword.

GRENADIER GUARDS.
Horse Equipments.

Saddle—usual hunting, with holsters covered with bearskin flounce.

Saddle-Cloth—blue cloth, three feet in length, one foot ten inches in depth, trimmed with two rows of one-inch regimental pattern gold lace, embroidered with star or crown according to rank. The Adjutant's saddle-cloth to have only one row of gold lace, without star or crown.

Bridle—black patent leather, with gilt buckles, à la Grec, bent branch bit, with gilt bosses, having V.R. in centre of garter, with laurel beneath and a crown over it; ring bridoon, with cheeks, blue front and rosettes.

Breastplate and Crupper—black patent leather with gilt bosses.

COLDSTREAM GUARDS.
Horse Equipment.

Saddle—usual hunting, with holsters covered with bearskin flounce.

Saddle-Cloth—same as Grenadier Guards, with two rows of one-inch regimental lace, with star or crown, according to rank. One row of gold lace for Adjutant, and without star or crown.

Bridle—plain black leather, with plated buckles, bent branch bit, with silver star bosses, having royal garter and crown, both gilt, in centre of boss.

Breastplate and Crupper—plain black leather, with a bunch of patent leather rosettes on each.

SCOTS FUSILIER GUARDS.
Horse Equipment.

Saddle—usual hunting, with holsters covered with bearskin flounce.

Saddle-Cloth—blue cloth, with two rows of gold lace seven-eighths wide, of regimental pattern, three feet wide at bottom, two feet two inches at top, one foot nine inches depth, with star or crown, according to rank. One row of gold lace for Adjutant, without star or crown.

Bridle—of black patent eather, with crossed face, mounted with gilt star ornament, having a silver thistle in centre; gilt wire whole buckles, gilt lion and crown in centre of noseband, and gilt ball and socket to throatband, with black hair throat ornament, whip to rein, bent branch bit, with gilt bosses, having a silver thistle in centre, blue front and rosettes.

Breastplate and Crupper—of black patent leather, made same as Infantry, with gilt bosses.

INFANTRY OF THE LINE.

Coat—tunic, scarlet, single-breasted, eight buttons in front at equal distances, with a fly one and three-quarters inch wide, thus buttoning well over; collar and cuffs of the regimental facing, the collar rounded off in front; the cuff ten and a half inches round, and two and three-quarters inches deep; a slashed flap on the sleeve, of the regimental facing, six inches long and two inches and a quarter wide, with three loops of half-inch lace, and regimental buttons. The skirt 10½ inches deep for an Officer five feet nine inches in height, with a variation of half an inch longer or shorter for every inch of difference in the height of the wearer. Scarlet flaps at the plaits behind, ten inches deep, two buttons on flap and one on waist, the two waist buttons standing three inches apart, with three loops of half-inch lace. The coat, collar, cuffs, and flaps edged with white cloth a quarter of an inch wide, and the skirts lined with white. On the left shoulder a crimson silk cord to retain the sash, with a regimental button.

The Field Officers to be distinguished by lace round the top and bottom of the collar, down the edge of the skirts behind, also on the edge of the skirt-flaps and edge of the sleeve-flaps; two rows of lace round the top of the cuffs; and the following badges embroidered in silver at each end of the collar, viz.:—

Colonel	. A crown and star.
Lieutenant-Colonel .	. A crown.
Major	. A star.

The other Officers to have lace on the top only of the collar, one row round the top of the cuff, none on the edge of the skirts; the loops only on the skirt-flaps and sleeve-flaps, and the following badges at each end of the collar.

  Captain . . . . A crown and star.
  Lieutenant . . . A crown.
  Ensign . . . . A star.

Lace—gold, according to the pattern established for each regiment, but in no case to exceed the breadth of half an inch.

Buttons—gilt, of uniform size of the sealed pattern with the regimental device throughout, except that on the shoulder, which is to be small.

Cap—chaco of black felt, five inches and a quarter deep in front, seven inches and an eighth deep behind, one inch less in diameter at top than at bottom; patent leather sunk top, turned over at the edge to the breadth of three-eighths of an inch, and stitched round; a band of the same, double stitched, and five-eighths of an inch wide, encircles the bottom of the cap; a peak of patent leather two inches and three-eighths wide in front, and another one inch and three-eighths wide behind; a chin-strap, three-quarters of an inch wide, fastened inside to the top of the cap; gilt plate, a star of eight points, three inches and five-eighths in extreme diameter, surmounted by a crown, and having the number of the regiment in bright gold on a black ground, within a garter proper; a bronze gorgon's head at the back for a ventilator.*

Worsted Ball Tuft†—two-thirds white, and one-third red, at the bottom, with a gilt socket.

---

* The Lieutenant-Colonel to be distinguished by two rows of regimental lace (showing a light of ¼ inch between) round the top of the chaco. The Majors to wear one row.

† The 34th Regiment has permission to wear a ball tuft half red and half white, the white uppermost.

The Light Company of the 46th have permission to wear a red ball tuft.

Stock—black silk.

Trousers—from the 15th of October to the 30th of April, Oxford mixture cloth, with a scarlet welt, quarter inch broad, down the outward seam; from the 1st of May to the 14th of October, dark blue with same scarlet welt; white linen, in the East Indies.

Boots—Wellington.

Spurs—for mounted Officers, screw, yellow metal, with crane necks, two inches long.

Sword—gilt half-basket hilt, with the Queen's cypher inserted in the outward bars, and lined with black patent leather; the gripe of black fish-skin, bound with a spiral of three gilt wires; length of the blade thirty-two inches and a half, width at the shoulder one inch and an eighth, and at twelve inches from the shoulder one inch; thickness of back at shoulder three-eighths of an inch, and at eighteen inches from the hilt, a quarter of an inch; solid flat shoulder an inch and a half deep, and blade hollowed from the flat to within nine inches of the point, which is spear-shaped; weight not less than one pound fifteen ounces without the scabbard.

Scabbard—for Regimental Field Officers, brass; for Adjutants, steel; for other Officers, black leather, with gilt mountings.

Sword-Knot—crimson and gold, strap, with acorn head.

Sword-Belt—of enamelled white leather an inch and a half wide, with slings and a gilt hook; the sword, when hooked up, to have the edge to the rear and the back to the front. This is to be the only sword-belt for all occasions. To be worn over the coat.

Plate—a round clasp, gilt, having on the centre piece the number of the regiment, surmounted by a crown, both in silver, and on the outer circle the regimental title in silver letters.

Sash—crimson silk net, with fringe ends, united by a crimson runner. Worn diagonally over the left shoulder, and over the sword-belt, and the ends of the fringe not to hang below the bottom of the coat.

Gloves—white leather.

Frock-Coat—blue, double-breasted, with stand-up collar rounded off in front; cuffs and lappels all blue. Round cuffs two inches and three-quarters deep, slash flap on sleeve five inches and a quarter long, one inch and a half wide, with three small regimental buttons. Two rows of regimental buttons down the front, eight in each row at equal distances, the distance between the rows eight inches at top and four inches at bottom; flaps behind ten inches deep, with two buttons on flap and one on waist; the skirt lined with black, and seventeen inches deep for an Officer five feet nine inches in height, with a variation of half an inch longer or shorter for each inch of difference in the height of the wearer. On the left shoulder, a crimson silk cord to retain the sash, with a small regimental button. Field Officers to have the distinction of their rank (crown and star for Colonels; crown, Lieut.-Colonel; star, Major), embroidered in gold at each end of the collar. The collars of the other Officers to be plain.

Forage-Cap—blue cloth, with black leather peak and chin-strap, of shape according to the pattern deposited at Army Clothing Department; band of black silk oak-leaf lace (except in "Royal" Regiments, where it is to be scarlet cloth), with the regimental number or distinction worked on the front in gold; the number to be one inch and a half long, placed on the band in front, black button and trimming on the top. Officers of the following regiments are permitted to wear the under-mentioned badges embroidered in addition to the number.

Boots in undress—Wellington or ankle.

The following regiments of Infantry are permitted to wear the under-mentioned badges in front of their caps, above the number of the regiment.

1st Royal Regiment	-	The Royal Cypher and Crown within the Collar and Garter of St. Andrew.
2nd or Queen's Royal	-	The Lamb.
3rd Buffs - -	-	The Dragon.
4th or King's Own	-	The Lion.
6th - - - -	-	The Antelope.
8th the King's -	-	The White Horse.
9th - - - -	-	Britannia.
18th Royal Irish -	-	The Harp and Crown.
27th Inniskilling -	-	A Castle.
33rd the Duke of Wellington's - - - -	-	Duke of Wellington's Crest,—a Demi-Lion rampant, out of a Ducal Coronet, and Scroll under.
54th - - - -	-	Sphinx, above the word "Marabout."
Fusilier Regiments	-	*vide* page 122.
Highland Regiments	-	*vide* page 123.

{Sealed patterns deposited at Army Clothing Department.}

All other regiments of the Line are to wear upon the forage-cap their proper *numbers* only.

Shell-Jacket—(when permitted to be worn, vide page 109,) scarlet, edged with white, with rounded collar and pointed cuffs, five inches in height, of regimental facing; and 10 small regimental buttons down the front at equal distances, and two on each sleeve. Field Officers distinguished by crown and star—crown—or star—in gold, on collar.

Cloak—a grey cloak coat with cape, according to pattern, of the same colour as the great coats of the men.

An oil-skin cover is permitted to be worn in bad weather both with the dress-cap and the forage-cap.

REGIMENTAL STAFF OFFICERS.

The Adjutant is to wear the uniform of his rank, and in the field a steel scabbard, steel spurs, crane neck, two inches long.

Paymasters, Quartermasters, Surgeons, and Assistant-Surgeons, are to wear the uniform of their respective regiments, with the distinctions of their corresponding ranks, excepting that they are to wear cocked hats, black waist-belts with slings, and no sash. The hat to be nine inches deep in the fan or back part, the front seven inches and a half, and each corner five inches, with loop of regimental lace, the same as worn on the coat, and crape-fringe tassels; the Paymaster to wear no feather; the Quartermaster to have a hackle feather five inches long; in Fusilier Regiments, all white; in regiments of the Line, three inches white and two inches red at the bottom; in Light Infantry Regiments, green; the Surgeon and Assistant-Surgeon to wear a feather of black cock's tail, drooping from a feathered stem three inches in length.

The Surgeon and Assistant-Surgeon will also wear a black shoulder-belt, with a small case of instruments, according to pattern.

LIGHT INFANTRY.

The dress and equipment of Officers of Light Infantry Regiments are to be the same as those of Officers of Infantry of the Line, with the following exceptions:—

Cap-Plate —a bugle inserted under the number of the regiment, as shown in a pattern deposited at the Office for Military Boards.

Plume—green horsehair, drooping from stem five inches high, with gilt ball socket, according to sealed pattern at Army Clothing Department.

Forage-Cap—dark green cloth, with black silk oak-leaf band; or, in regiments styled "Royal," a red cloth band. Black leather peak and chin-strap. Gold embroidered bugle above the number, with black button and trimming on the top. Rifle Regiments and Highland Light Infantry wear the green ball as heretofore.

FUSILIERS.

The dress and equipment of Officers of Fusilier Regiments are to be the same with those of Officers of Infantry of the Line, with the following exceptions:—

Cap-Plate—a grenade, bearing the badge of the regiment, as shown in patterns deposited at the Army Clothing Department.

Plume—white horsehair, drooping from stem five inches high, with gilt grenade socket, except the 5th or Northumberland Fusiliers, who are authorized to wear one of red and white, the red uppermost—patterns deposited at Army Clothing Department.

Forage-Cap—blue cloth, with black leather peak and chin-strap, and a red cloth band, with thereon the number of the regiment embroidered in gold, surmounted by a gold embroidered grenade, having on the centre of the ball the following distinctions for each Regiment, viz.:—

5th Fusiliers - - St. George and the Dragon in silver.
7th Royal Fusiliers - The Rose   ,,
21st R. N. B Fusiliers, The Thistle   ,,
23rd R. Welsh Fusiliers, The Red Dragon   ,,

87th R. Irish Fusiliers, Prince of Wales' Plume and Harp in silver. Patterns deposited at Army Clothing Department.

Note.—The Officers of the 23rd, or Royal Welsh Fusiliers, have permission to wear "*the flash.*"

HIGHLAND REGIMENTS.

Jacket—scarlet, single-breasted, with eight buttons at equal distances, and a fly one and three-quarters inch wide, thus buttoning well over; collar and cuffs of the regimental facings, the collar two inches high and rounded off in front. The cuff ten and a half inches round, two and three-quarters inches deep, and a slashed flap on the sleeve, of the colour of the regimental facings, with three buttons and loops of gold braid. Shoulder straps of plain gold double cord, with a small regimental button. Double Inverness skirts six inches and a half deep; skirt flaps with three buttons and loops of gold braid; the skirt and skirt-flaps lined with white. An edging of white one quarter of an inch wide all round the jacket, cuffs, and flaps.

The Field Officers have an edging of half-inch lace to the sleeve-slash, skirts, and skirt-flaps and round the top and bottom of the collar, and two rows on the top of the cuff; and also the following distinctions at each end of the collar:—

Colonel, a crown and star.

Lieutenant-Colonel, a crown.

Major, a star.

The other Officers have half-inch lace round the top of the collar, one row of the same round the top of the cuff, and the following distinctions at each end of the collar:—

Captain, a crown and star.
Lieutenant, a crown.
Ensign, a star.

Lace—gold, according to the patterns established for each regiment, but in no case to exceed the breadth of half an inch.

Buttons—as for Infantry with regimental device.

Bonnet—cocked and feathered with six black ostrich feathers, twelve inches deep; skull, of Tartan plaid; a rosette, with regimental button or badge, on the left side; black leather chin-strap.

Feather—white vulture, eight inches long.

Belted Plaid
Kilt
Purse
Hose
Garters
Shoes and Buckles
} According to Highland costume, and to established regimental patterns.

Or *Trews*—of the regimental Tartan, with Wellington boots, on those occasions on which the kilt is not worn.

Sword—Highland, with steel hilt, lined with scarlet cloth, straight cut-and-thrust blade, one inch and a half wide at the shoulder, and thirty-two inches long.

Scabbard—black leather with steel mountings; steel in the field for Regimental Field Officers.

Sword-Belt—for Regimental Field Officers, *Waist-Belt*; for other Officers, *Shoulder-Belt*, three inches wide, with slings, all of white enamelled leather.

Breast-Plate
Dirk
} of established regimental pattern.

Sash—crimson silk net, with fringe ends and crimson runner, worn diagonally over the left shoulder.

Scarf—according to regimental pattern, to be worn with the scarlet jacket on occasions when the kilt is not worn.

Stock—black silk.

Gloves—white leather.

Shell-Jacket—as prescribed for Officers of Infantry of the Line.

Frock-Coat
Cloak
Spurs, for mounted Officers
} As prescribed for Officers of Infantry of the Line.

Forage-Cap—to be of blue cloth (if Light Infantry, to be green) with red seam round crown; band to be of regimental Tartan; the number of the regiment in gold embroidery on the band and a gold embroidered thistle above the number; a black leather peak and chin-strap.

The 42nd Highlanders—to have the St. Andrew Badge upon the thistle.

The 72nd Highlanders—to have a small star upon the thistle.

The 71st Highlanders—to have a gold embroidered horn bugle with a small thistle in centre, above the gold number.

Sword-Belt—black leather, with gilt mountings and slings; but the sword is on no account to be allowed to trail on the ground; to be worn only with the blue frock-coat.

The 42nd Regiment is permitted to wear a Scarlet vulture feather, eight inches long.

The 71st Highland Light Infantry and the 74th Regiment are each permitted to wear a Tartan plaid scarf, and a special Cap of regimental pattern, deposited at Army Clothing Department.

The 71st, 72nd, and 74th wear the trews on all occasions.

REGIMENTAL STAFF.

The Adjutant is to wear the uniform of his rank: in the field steel scabbard, and steel spurs, crane neck, two inches long.

The Paymaster, Quartermaster, Surgeon, and Assistant-Surgeon are to wear the same uniform as the other Officers, excepting that the feather is to be *black* for the Surgeon and Assistant-Surgeon; the *Sash* is not to be worn; the waist-belt with slings is to be worn on all occasions, and under the jacket. The Regimental Staff are not required to wear the plaid and kilt.

RIFLE REGIMENTS.

Distinctions of Rank.

Colonel, crown and star.
Lieutenant-Colonel, crown
Major, star.
 { Collar laced all round with black lace, figured braiding within the lace.
  Sleeve ornament, lace and figured braiding eleven inches deep.

Captain, crown and star.
 { Collar laced round the top with black lace, with figured braiding below the lace.
  Sleeve ornament, knot of square cord with figured braiding eight inches deep.

Lieutenant, crown.
Ensign, star
 { Collar laced round the top with black lace and plain edging of braid.
  Sleeve ornament, knot of square cord and braid seven inches deep.

The collar badges in silk embroidery.

Jacket—tunic, rifle green, with collar and cuffs of regimental facings; single-breasted; the collar rounded in front. On each side of the breast five loops of black square cord, with netted caps and drops, fastening with worked olivets; the top loop eight inches long, the bottom one four inches. A double cord on the shoulders, with small regimental button. The jacket edged all round (except the collar) with black square cord. On the back seams, a single cord forming three eyes at the top, passing under a netted cap at the waist, below which it is doubled, and terminating in a knot at the bottom of skirt. The skirt nine inches deep for an Officer five feet nine inches in height, with the variations of half an inch for every inch of difference in height, and lined with black, and rounded off in front.*

The facings of the 60th Royal Rifles, and of the Royal Canadian Rifle Regiment, are of scarlet cloth; those of the Rifle Brigade and of the Ceylon Rifle Regiment, of black velvet.

Cap—the same as for Infantry of the Line; but, instead of a plate, a bronze bugle surmounted by a black silk cord rosette, in the centre of which is a small bronze crown.†

Tuft—a black silk ball and slide.

Stock—black silk.

Trousers—rifle green cloth, with a braid of black mohair, two inches wide, down the outward seam; or, for summer wear, green gambroon, plain.‡

---

* The Officers of the Royal Canadian Rifle Regiment are permitted to wear, on parades and barrack duties, a plain green frock-coat, corresponding with the blue frock-coat of the Infantry of the Line, with buttons of black horn, and shoulder-straps of treble-plaited black silk cord, worked to the shape of a bugle at bottom. They have also a grey great coat, made double-breasted with grey fur collar and cuffs.

† The Officers of the 60th, or "King's Royal Rifle Corps," are permitted to wear a Maltese cross cap-plate, bearing the number and the bugle according to regimental pattern.

‡ In the Royal Canadian Rifle Regiment the dress trousers are trimmed down the outer seams with two stripes of half-inch black braid on a scarlet ground, showing a light and edging of scarlet; and the undress trousers with one stripe of black braid.

The Officers of the Ceylon Rifle Regiment are permitted to wear white linen trousers on ordinary occasions.

Boots—Wellington.

Spurs—steel, crane neck, two inches long.

Sword—the same as prescribed for Officers of Infantry of the Line, except that the hilt and mountings are of steel, and the device is a crown and bugle.

Scabbard—steel.

Sword-Knot—black leather.

Sword-Belt—black leather, one inch and a half wide, with slings, silver snake clasp and mountings, worn over the coat.

Pouch—black patent leather, with a silver bugle on the flap.

Pouch-Belt—black patent leather, three inches wide, with silver regimental plate. Patterns of regimental breastplate of Rifle Brigade and 60th R. Rifles are deposited at Army Clothing Department, whistle, and chain.

Gloves—black leather.

Forage-Cap—rifle green cloth, perfectly plain, black leather peak, and chin-strap.

Boots in undress—Wellington or ankle.

A Cap-Cover of oil-skin is permitted to be worn in bad weather, both with the dress-cap and the forage-cap.

Cloak—a grey cloak coat, according to the pattern established for the Infantry of the Line, of the same colour as the great coats of the men.

REGIMENTAL STAFF.

The Adjutant is to wear the uniform of his rank.

The Paymaster, Quartermaster, Surgeon, and Assistant-Surgeon are to wear a plain chaco ; no tuft. The Medical Officers, instead of the regimental pouch and belt, wear a black shoulder-belt, with a small case of instruments, according to pattern.

HORSE FURNITURE
FOR
MOUNTED OFFICERS OF INFANTRY.

Saddle—hunting.

Saddle-Cloth—of the same colour as the facing of the regiment, two feet ten inches in length, and one foot ten inches in depth. The saddle cloth of a Field Officer to be trimmed with one row of half-inch regimental lace, the same as worn on his coat, edged with a small vandyke of scarlet cloth, and the badge of his army rank, according to the Infantry regulation, embroidered in silver on the corners. The Adjutant's saddle-cloth to be trimmed only with a gold cord edged with a small vandyke of scarlet cloth.

Bridle—of black leather; bent branch bit, with gilt bosses, having the rose, thistle, and shamrock in the centre, encircled with the words—"*Infantry Mounted Officers,*" and the crown above: front and roses to correspond in colour with the facing of the regiment.

Holsters—to be covered with black bear-skin, except in tropical climates, where they are to be covered with *black patent leather.*

Saddle-cloth for mounted Officers of Rifle regiments to be green; for Field Officers, to be trimmed with half-inch lace of regimental pattern. Field Officers to have on saddle cloth the distinctive braiding of their rank, as on the tunic. Adjutants to be trimmed with cord of rifle green.

Bridle as for the rest of infantry, with green front and roses, and bronze bosses. For mounted Officers of the Rifle Brigade, a shabraque of black lambskin, three feet four inches long, twenty-one inches deep in front, and twelve inches behind, with rounded corners in front and rear.

UNIFORM FOR OFFICERS OF CAPE MOUNTED RIFLES.

Distinctions of Rank.

DRESS.

Colonel, crown and star. *Lieutenant-Colonel*, crown. *Lieutenant*, star.	Collar laced all round with black lace, a figured braiding within the lace. Sleeve ornament of inch and a half black lace, and braid eleven inches deep.
Captain, crown and star.	Collar laced round the top with black lace a figured braiding below the lace. Sleeve ornament, knot of square cord and figured braid eight inches deep.
Lieutenant, crown. *Ensign*, star.	Collar laced round the top with black braid, with a plain edging of braid below the lace. Sleeve ornament, knot of square cord and narrow braid seven inches deep.

The collar badges in black silk embroidery.

Jacket—tunic, rifle green, black cloth collar and cuffs, the collar rounded in front and ornamented with black mohair three quarter-inch lace and braid; on each side of the breast five loops of black square cord with netted caps and drops fastened with worked olivets, the top loop eight inches long, the bottom one four inches long; a double cord on the shoulder, and with small netted buttons. The tunic edged all round, except the collar, with black square cord; on the back seam a single cord forming three eyes at the top, passing under a netted cap at the waist, below which it is doubled, and terminating in a knot at the bottom of the skirt; the skirt nine inches deep, for an officer five feet nine inches in height, with variation of half an inch for every inch of difference in height, and lined with black, and rounded off in front.

Cap—chaco, of black felt nine inches deep at the back, and five and a quarter inches in front, sunk tip, black patent leather peak, with black braid laid on flat all round, three quarter-inch wide and edged; black one and three quarter-inch lace round top of chaco; bronzed metal cross and crown over, chain, roses, and gorgon's head at the back for a ventilator.

Cap-Line—black silk with acorn ends.

Plume—black horse hair and bronzed metal socket.

Stock—black silk.

Trousers—dark green cloth, cut wide at the thighs with side pockets; two-inch black mohair braid down outward seam, and strapped with the same between the legs.

Forage-Cap—rifle green cloth, perfectly plain, black leather peak embroidered with black mohair and chin-strap according to sealed pattern deposited at Army Clothing Department.

Boots—Wellington.

Spurs—steel, crane neck, two inches long.

Sabre—As for cavalry.

Scabbard—steel.

Sword-Knot—black leather.

Sword-Belt—black leather one and a half inch wide with slings; a silver snake clasp and mountings.

Pouch-Belt—black patent leather three inches wide, with a silver eight-pointed star and crown over, and wreath of laurel encircling C.M.R. in the centre of star, whistle and chain, and pickers.

Pouch—black patent leather, with silver letters *C.M.R.* on the flap.

Gloves—black leather.

Cloak—grey cloth (same as used for infantry regiments) with sleeves, and hand pockets in front, bronzed rose clasp and bronzed buttons; a detached cape of the same cloth.

HORSE FURNITURE.

Bridle—as for rifle regiments.

Saddle-Cloth—as for rifle regiments, with the letters C.M.R. embroidered in black on the corners.

Saddle—as for Officers of cavalry.

Valise—ditto.

WEST INDIA REGIMENTS.

Uniform same as for Infantry.

Forage-Cap—to have "W.I.R." on band, and gold embroidered number above the letters.

ROYAL NEWFOUNDLAND COMPANIES.

Uniform same as for Infantry.

Forage Cap—to have a gold embroidered R.N.C. on the band.

ROYAL MALTA FENCIBLES.

Uniform same as for Infantry.

Forage-Cap—to have a gold embroidered V.R. and Crown on the band and Maltese star above.

OFFICERS OF THE CORPS OF INSTRUCTORS OF MUSKETRY.

STAFF OF THE SCHOOL OF MUSKETRY.

COMMANDANT AND INSPECTOR-GENERAL OF INSTRUCTION,

AND

CHIEF INSTRUCTOR (FIELD OFFICERS).

Uniform and appointments the same as for Colonel on the Staff, lace to be of the pattern established for Royal Regiments, badge of respective ranks on the collar; the buttons to have the device of cross muskets, as per pattern at Clothing Department.

CAPTAINS INSTRUCTORS
AND
LIEUTENANT AND DEPUTY ASSISTANT ADJUTANT-GENERAL.

Uniform and appointments as for Staff Captains, with button of the corps, and badge of the respective ranks. Lace as before described.

CORPS OF INSTRUCTORS.
DISTRICT INSPECTORS (CAPTAINS).

Tunic—as for Officers of the line, single-breasted, eight buttons up the front, the edges of the coat, collar, cuffs and flaps, to be edged with quarter inch white cassimere, the collar, cuffs and sleeve slashes to be of blue cloth, the lace as for Royal Regiments, with the button of the corps.

Other articles of dress and appointments the same as the Officers of the line, the chaco and waist plates as per patterns at Army Clothing Department.

Forage-Cap—blue cloth, with red band and cross muskets thereon, in gold embroidery.

Horse Furniture—same as for Garrison Staff.

GOLD COAST ARTILLERY.

Uniform and appointments as for Officers of Infantry, with blue facings. Chaco, and waist-plates, and button as in pattern at Army Clothing Department.

UNATTACHED OFFICERS
AND
OFFICERS ON HALF-PAY.

Coat—tunic, scarlet, single-breasted, with blue collar, cuffs. The collar rounded at the corners. The cuff round ten and a-half inches and two inches and three quarters deep; scarlet slashed flap on the sleeve, six inches long and two inches and a quarter wide, with three buttons, and twist loops. Eight buttons down the front at equal distances. The skirt $10\frac{1}{2}$ inches deep for an Officer five feet nine inches in height, with a variation of half an inch longer or shorter for each inch of difference in the height of the wearer. Scarlet flap on the skirt behind, ten inches deep, two buttons on flap and one on waist, with three twist loops. The coat, collar, cuffs, and flaps edged with white, and the skirts lined with white. On the left shoulder a crimson silk cord, to retain the sash, with a small button.

The rank of each Officer to be distinguished as in the Infantry of the Line, viz.:—

Field Officers by an edging of lace on the top and bottom of the collar, on the sleeve and skirt flaps, and down the skirts behind, two rows of lace on the top of the cuff, and their proper badges at each end of the collar.

The other Officers to have lace on the top of the collar only, with their proper badges at each end, and one row of lace on the top of the cuff.

Lace—gold, two-vellum pattern, half-inch width.

Button—gilt, convex, with a raised crown and scalloped edge, of before prescribed size and form.

Hat—cocked; the fan or back part nine inches deep, the front seven inches and a half, each corner five inches; gold lace loop, and tassels of gold crape fringe, with crimson crape fringe underneath.

Feather—white upright hackle, five inches long.

Trousers—as prescribed for Officers of infantry.

Boots—Wellington.

Spurs—for Field Officers, screw, yellow metal, with necks two inches long, including rowels.

Sword—the same as for Officers of infantry.

Scabbard—black leather, with gilt mountings.

Sword-Knot—crimson and gold, with acorn tassel.

Sword-Belt—white enamelled leather, with slings, worn over the coat.

Plate—a round gilt clasp, with the cypher V.R. and a crown on the centre-piece, and the word "Unattached" on the outer circle.

Sash—crimson silk net, with fringe ends and a crimson runner, worn diagonally over the left shoulder.

Blue Frock-Coat—as prescribed for Officers of infantry.

Stock—black silk.

Gloves—white leather.

Forage-Cap—same as for infantry Officers, without number or device.

Officers who are reduced to Half-Pay, in consequence of a reduction of the establishment of their Regiment, or in consequence of the entire disbandment of their Regiment, may appear at Court in the uniform of the Regiment from which they were reduced. All Officers on Half-Pay, from any other causes whatever, are to appear in the uniform allotted to Unattached Officers.

Officers who have retired on Full-Pay, and Officers who have left the army, but whose names are allowed to remain in the Army List, are to wear the same uniform as Unattached Officers, with a black waist-belt instead of a white one.

ROYAL ARTILLERY.

GENERAL AND STAFF OFFICERS

Are to wear the dress and appointments laid down for their respective ranks by Her Majesty's Regulations.

Staff Officers are to conform to the same Regulations, with the exception that, if employed on the Staff of the Artillery, the colour of the coat is to be blue, with scarlet collar and cuffs, and they are to wear the dress appointments ordered for the Officers of the Royal Artillery.

ROYAL HORSE ARTILLERY
AND
RIDING HOUSE ESTABLISHMENT.

Distinctions of Rank.

DRESS.

Colonel, crown and star. *Lieutenant-Colonel*, crown. *Regimental-Major*.	Collar laced all round with gold lace inside the gold cord. Chevron of flat gold lace one inch and a half wide, with three rows of small gold braid outside of chevron, two rows figured and centre one plain, eleven inches deep.
Captain, crown and star. *Lieutenant*, crown.	Collar laced round the top with gold lace within the gold cord. Sleeve ornament, Austrian knot of royal gold cord traced in and out with small gold braid, eight inches deep and figured for Captains, seven inches deep and plain for Lieutenants.

The collar badges to be in silver embroidery.

The dress uniform is to be worn at Levees and Drawing-rooms, on birth days, and in review order.

The undress uniform is for general use, and to be worn on all occasions not otherwise specified.

The blue frock-coat may be worn with the forage cap as a common morning dress in quarters; in this dress the sword belt without sabretache is to be worn under the coat.

Stable jacket to be worn at all drills, parades, and duties when the men appear in the stable dress or drill order, and it may also be worn at the regimental mess.

The forage-cap is to be worn on all mounted and dismounted parades when the men have on their forage caps, and on all occasions as an ordinary morning head-dress.

Upon no occasion is an Officer to appear in regimentals without his sword.

DRESS.

Jacket—dark blue edged all round with round gold cord; scarlet collar rounded in front, and edged all round with royal gold cord, loops of royal gold cord ($1\frac{3}{8}$ inches apart from centre to centre) on the breast; ball buttons with three guns and crown. Austrian knot of royal gold cord at each side of waist, and stripe of same up back seams, terminating in a crow's-foot at each shoulder. Round cord shoulder strap. Skirts of cavalry length, and with usual variation.

Busby—black sable skin eight inches high, scarlet bag, gold lines with acorns, leather chin-strap.

Plume—of egret feathers, nine inches in length.

Stock—black silk.

Trousers—dark blue cloth, with a stripe of gold lace, regimental pattern, one inch and three-quarters wide, down the outward seams.

Boots—Wellington.

Spurs—yellow metal, swan neck two inches long, including rowels; for Court and full dress only.

Sword—Regulation, Light Cavalry.

Scabbard—steel.

Sword-Knot—gold line, with an acorn.

Sword-Belt—blue Morocco leather covered with gold lace one inch wide, with slings without swivels, united with two small plates, crown surmounted by lion, S hook fastening, with motto " Ubique " on the fastenings.

Sabretache—blue Morocco, faced with blue cloth, with broad gold lace round it; within, embroidered, the Royal Arms and supporters, a cannon below, with the motto " Ubique" above, and " Quo fas et gloria ducunt" below it.

Pouch—blue Morocco leather, five inches and a half long, two inches and a quarter deep, and one inch wide; outside leaf dark blue cloth lined with blue Morocco. Stripe of three quarters of an inch flat gold lace round outer edge. Embroidered gun, and motto " Ubique," surmounted by the Royal Arms and supporters, encircled with wreath of oak and laurel leaves; underneath, " Quo fas et gloria ducunt." Gilt buckle ring, and stud, with leaf on each end.

Pouch-Belt—blue Morocco (in two pieces), covered with gold lace on the short piece; gilt ornamental buckles, and slide and fuze encircled with wreath at the end of long piece.

Gloves—white leather.

UNDRESS.

Frock-Coat—dark blue cloth, single-breasted, rounded with collar in front and edged with black mohair square cord, six loops of black mohair square cord, and six olivets in front of the coat on the breast, and terminating with crow's-feet. The ornaments on the skirt are also of black mohair square cord; crow's-foot on each side of the back at the waist, with two loops extending from them eight inches down the skirt, with crow's-foot at the end of each. The rank of the Officer to be shown on the sleeve, in like manner as on the jacket, but in black cord and lace, and Field Officer to wear distinctive badge on collar in gold.

Forage-Cap—dark blue cloth, with patent leather straight peak, band of gold lace one inch and seven tenths wide (regimental pattern); a convex gold button on the crown.

Trousers—dark blue cloth, with a scarlet stripe one inch and three quarters wide, down the outward seams.

Stable-Jacket—blue, single-breasted, scarlet collar, gold Russia braid all round the collar and jacket, terminating at each hip in a figure of 8; sleeves trimmed according to rank; holes and buttons down front one and three quarters inches apart; two buttons at each wrist; lining white. Field Officer to wear distinctive badge on collar.

Sword-Belt—black patent leather, one and one-eighth inch wide, gilt S hook fastening, with Royal crest on either side, and the motto "Ubique" on the fastening.

Sabretache—black patent leather, the badge gilt, royal arms and supporters, with motto "Ubique" and gun beneath; "Quo fas et gloria ducunt" beneath all.

Pouch—black patent leather, six inches and three quarters long, two inches and three quarters deep, and one inch and a half wide; outside leaf eight inches deep, six inches and one-eighth wide at back, and seven inches and three quarters in front, rounded at the ends and wavy; gilt device, gun, buckle, ring and stud, with leaf at each end; to contain a small field telescope, scale, pair of compasses, and pencil.

Pouch-Belt—same as dress.

Spurs—steel, swan neck, two inches long, including rowels.

Boots,
Sword,
Scabbard, } the same as in dress.
Sword-Knot,
Stock,
Gloves,

Cloak—dark blue cloth with sleeves; cape twenty-four inches deep, lined with white; collar scarlet on both sides; seven regimental buttons down the front.

Note—The Quarter-Master to wear the dress prescribed for Lieutenants.

HORSE FURNITURE.

Shabracque—dark blue cloth, with gold lace two inches wide round the edges, with a crown and the Royal cypher; a gun on the flaps, with the motto " Ubique " underneath; the ends of the flaps to be rounded off.

Undress—black Ukraine lambskin, edged scarlet.

Bridle—of brown leather, with cross face and top cross ornamented with leather rosettes of the same, bent branch bit with swivel, top eyes, gilt bosses with lion upon crown (Ubique) underneath, with garter and motto round, and crown above link and the bridoon.

Breastplate and Crupper—of brown leather ornamented with rosettes of the same.

IN MARCHING ORDER.

Cloak—rolled three feet long under the sheepskin in front of the saddle.

Valise—dark blue cloth, with round ends edged with gold cord, and R.H.A. in gold cord at each end.

ROYAL ARTILLERY.

BATTALIONS.

Distinctions of Rank.

DRESS.

Colonel, crown and star. *Lieutenant-Colonel,* crown. *Serjeant-Major,* star.	Collar laced all round with gold lace inside the gold cord. Chevron of flat gold lace one inch and a half wide, with three rows of small gold braid outside of chevron, two rows figured, and centre one plain, eleven inches deep.
Captain, crown and star. *Lieutenant,* crown.	Collar laced round the top with gold lace within the gold cord. Sleeve ornament, Austrian knot of royal gold cord traced in and out with small gold braid, eight inches deep and figured for Captains, seven inches deep and plain for Lieutenants.

The collar badge to be in silver embroidery.

Tunic—dark blue cloth. Scarlet collar rounded in front, edged all round with Royal gold cord. Buttons of size and form prescribed for infantry (with three guns and crown), two inches and a quarter between each down the front, two on each sleeve and two on the hip; edged all round, and up skirt seams with scarlet. Skirt ten inches and a half deep for an officer six feet in height, with usual variations, rounded in front, round gold cord shoulder-cord.

Busby—black sable skin eight inches high, scarlet bag to hang over the right side, and hooked down to the busby; leather chin-strap, and gilt grenade on the left side, to hold the plume.

Plume—of white goats' hair, six inches in length, to be worn on the left side of the busby.

Stock—black silk.

Trousers—dress—dark blue cloth, gold lace stripe (regimental pattern), one inch and three-quarters wide, down the outer seam; with pockets.

Boots—Wellington.

Spurs—dress and undress same as Royal Horse Artillery.

Sword—regulation, Light Cavalry, for all ranks.

Scabbard—steel.

Sword-Knot—gold cord, with acorn.

Sword-Belt—dress—blue Morocco leather, covered with gold lace, one inch wide, with slings, without swivels, united with two small plates. Crown surmounted by lion, S hook fastening, with motto "Ubique" on the fastenings.

Undress—white patent leather, one inch and seven tenths wide, with slings; plate, gilt; device, the royal arms, encircled with a wreath of the rose, shamrock, and thistle, surmounted by a crown, and with the motto "Ubique" beneath.

Sabretache, for Adjutants — undress—black patent leather, the badge gilt; royal arms and supporters, with motto, "Ubique," gun beneath, and "Quo fas et gloria ducunt" beneath all.

Gloves—white leather.

Frock-Coat—same as for Royal Horse Artillery.

Forage-Cap—
Cloak— } same as for Royal Horse Artillery.

Stable-Jacket—same as for Royal Horse Artillery.

Trousers—undress—dark blue cloth, with scarlet stripe, one inch and three-quarters wide, down the outer seam.

Pouch—dress—blue morocco leather, five inches and a half long, two inches and a quarter deep, one inch wide; outside leaf dark blue cloth, lined with blue Morocco leather, stripe of three-quarter inch flat gold lace round outer edge; embroidered gun, and motto "Ubique," surmounted by the royal arms and supporters, encircled with a wreath of oak and laurel leaves; underneath, " Quo fas et gloria ducunt;" gilt buckle, ring, and stud with leaf on each end.

Undress—black patent leather, six inches and three quarters long, two inches and three quarters deep, one inch and a half wide; outside leaf, eight inches deep, six inches and seven eighths wide at back, and seven inches and three-quarters in front, rounded at the ends, and wavy; device, gilt, gun; buckle, ring, and stud, with leaf at each end; to contain a small field telescope, scale, pair of compasses, and pencil.

Pouch-Belt—dress—blue Morocco leather, in two pieces, covered with gold lace; on the short piece, gilt ornamental buckle and slide; fuse, encircled with wreath, on short piece.

Undress—white patent leather, two inches wide.

REGIMENTAL STAFF OFFICERS.

The Medical Officers of the Royal Artillery are to conform to the dress laid down for Officers of corresponding rank in the battalions of Royal Artillery, viz. :

Senior Surgeons as Field Officers.
Surgeons as Captains.
Assistant Surgeons as Lieutenants, except that they are to wear the regulation cocked hat and plume.

The Quarter-Masters are to wear the dress prescribed for Lieutenants, with the cocked hat instead of the busby.

The Veterinary Surgeons as Medical Officers of corresponding rank.

ROYAL ENGINEERS.

GENERAL AND STAFF OFFICERS.

General Officers are to wear the dress and appointments, as laid down for their respective ranks by Her Majesty's Regulations of the 1st April 1855.

Staff Officers are to conform to the Regulations for the dress of the Staff of the Army, except that in full dress they will wear the regimental collar and shoulder knot, and that the sleeve ornament of the *Assistant Adjutant-General* be that ordered for Field Officers of the Corps, and of a *Brigade Major* (if not a Field Officer) a similar device, but with one row only of figured braiding above the chevron.

Facings of garter blue velvet.

The lace on the trousers, cocked hat, &c., to be of the regimental pattern.

The plume to be of the regimental shape and size, with scarlet and white feathers mixed.

The undress and *all* appointments to be of the regimental pattern, and to be worn as herein directed; except that the peak of the forage cap is to be embroidered.

BADGE of the CORPS of ROYAL ENGINEERS and ROYAL SAPPERS AND MINERS.

The Royal Arms and Supporters, with the Mottoes,
Ubique;
Quo fas et gloria ducunt;
(underneath).

ROYAL ENGINEERS.

Distinctions of Rank.

DRESS.

Colonel, crown and star.
Lieutenant-Colonel, star.
Regimental-Major, crown.

{ Collar laced all round with gold lace inside the gold cord.
Chevron of flat gold regimental lace (corps pattern) with three rows of small gold braid outside of chevron, two rows figured, and centre row plain, eleven inches deep.

Captain, crown and star.
Lieutenant, crown.

{ Collar laced round the top with gold lace inside the gold cord.
Sleeve ornament, Austrian knot of round back gold cord traced in and out with small gold braid eight inches deep, and figured for Captains; seven inches deep and plain for Lieutenants.

The collar badge to be in silver embroidery.

Tunic—Scarlet cloth, edged with blue velvet, single-breasted, buttons 2 inches asunder. Collar and cuffs of garter blue velvet.

Round-back gold cord on edge of collar and collar seam, skirt plain, and lined with white kerseymere; 12 inches long for an officer 5 feet 9 inches in height, with ½ an inch more or less for each inch of difference in height.

K

Sleeve—not to exceed 10½ inches in circumference at the wrist, and to have distinctive ornaments as follows:—

Shoulder-Knot—Round-back gold cord, treble twist, with silver grenade (embroidered).

Hat—Cocked (corps pattern), with tassels of small gold bullion corners 4¾ inches long, ends 2½ inches broad, fan 7½ inches high, front flap 6¾ inches high, with a loop of gold lace (corps pattern) 1 inch wide; small regimental button, and watered ribbon cockade, ribbon on sides, front and rear plain.

N.B. Officers appointed to companies to wear the same head-dress as the men, when paraded with them. The men wear busby with blue bag and white plume, pattern deposited at Army Clothing Department.

Feather—White cock, 5¼ inches long, mushroom shape.

Trousers, Dress—dark Oxford mixture, gold lace stripe (corps pattern), 1¾ inches wide down outer seam.

Sword—Regulation pattern blade for infantry, 32½ inches long by 1⅛ inch wide; hilt of rolled metal, gilt, scroll pattern, pierced and engraved.

Scabbard for Field Officers—brass.

For other ranks—steel.

Sword-Knot—Round gold cord, with acorn.

Sword-Belt—(to be worn over the coat) Russia leather, 1½ inches wide, two stripes of gold embroidery ¼ inch wide; plain gilt buckles, carriages embroidered on both sides; gilt plate, with corps' device in silver.

Boots—Wellington.

Spurs—Brass, crane neck, 2 inches long, including rowels.

Gloves—White leather.

Stock—Black silk or patent leather.

Pouch-Belt—Russia leather, 2¼ inches wide, one stripe of gold embroidery, ⅜ inch wide on either edge, and one in a scroll down the centre. Buckle tip and slide gilt and engraved.

Pouch—Black patent leather, regimental badge gilt on outside leaf.

Box, 5 inches long, $2\frac{1}{4}$ inches deep, and $1\frac{1}{2}$ inches wide.

UNDRESS.

Frock-Coat—Blue cloth, single-breasted, rolling collar, to hook-and-eye up to 5 inches from bottom of stock.

8 loops of $\frac{3}{4}$ inch braid (mohair) down front, and 2 rows of netted barrels on each side.

Front edges and collar, back seams, and hind arm trimmed with $\frac{7}{8}$ inch braid and traced, two streamers of $\frac{7}{8}$ inch braid 8 inches long on each skirt, traced, and finished with points and crows-feet.

Cuffs pointed five inches deep of one inch braid, traced and finished with crows-feet; an extra row of small figured braiding on the cuff of a Captain, and the tracing of the cuff of a Field Officer to be as on the tunic. Field Officer to wear the relative collar badge.

Jacket—Scarlet cloth, single-breasted, with gilt studs down front to hook-and-eye ; plain gold braid all round, and on collar seam, finished with a crows-foot at centre of waist and collar seam ; shoulder cord, a single twist ; collar, garter blue velvet, rounded in front; cuffs, garter blue velvet, pointed five inches deep. If for a Lieutenant, edged with plain gold braid, a crows-foot at point. For a Captain an additional row of small figured braiding. For a Field Officer a chevron of gold lace, corps pattern (one inch wide), edged with plain braid and crows-feet at points, and the relative collar badge.

Waistcoat— Scarlet cloth, single-breasted, with gilt studs down front to hook and eye, plain gold braid all round on collar, seam, and pockets, finished with a crows-foot at each end of pockets.

Trousers—dark Oxford mixture, a scarlet stripe $1\frac{3}{4}$ inches wide down outer seam.

White linen or Russia drill on foreign stations in summer.

Forage-Cap—Blue cloth, a gold netted button in centre of crown, which is in eight parts, and edged with scarlet piping.

Band of gold lace, 1¾ inches wide (corps pattern), projecting peak; oilskin cover may be worn in wet weather.

Pouch-Belt—bridle leather, 1½ inches wide, with similar buckle and mountings.

Sword-Belt—bridle leather, 1½ inches wide, with similar plate and mountings.

Sketching-Case—Black patent leather, fitted up to contain drawing materials, to be attached to sword-belt by three corresponding narrow slings, regimental badge, &c., gilt.

To be worn only by Officers when employed in the field, but never in evening dress.

Great-Coat—Blue cloth, with cape and sleeves, lined with scarlet; upright scarlet cloth collar, with gilt clasps, chain, and grenades.

HORSE FURNITURE.
Saddle Cloth.

Dark blue cloth, 2 feet 10 inches long, each flap 1 foot 10 inches deep; one row of gold lace (corps pattern) 1 inch wide on scarlet cloth round outer edge.

Field Officers to have the badge of their army rank at each corner.

Bridle.

Bridle—of brown leather and cross-face piece, ornamented with rosettes of the same; bent branch bit with gilt bosses, having V. R. in the centre encircled with the words "Royal Engineers" and a crown above; front and rosettes of garter blue velvet.

Breastplate and Crupper—of brown leather ornamented with rosettes of the same.

Head-Collar—of brown leather with steel collar chain.

Brown leather wallets covered with black bearskin, except in tropical climates, where they are to be covered with black patent leather.

REGIMENTAL STAFF OFFICERS.

Adjutants—to wear the dress and appointments as ordered for their respective ranks.

Quarter-Masters—the dress and appointments to assimilate in every respect to those of the Subaltern Officers of Royal Engineers, except that the sword and pouch belts are to be of white patent leather, with gilt buckles and mountings.

UNATTACHED OFFICERS,

AND

OFFICERS ON HALF-PAY and ON THE RETIRED LIST.

To wear the dress prescribed for Officers of corresponding rank in the battalions of Artillery, substituting the regulation cocked hat for the busby.

HORSE FURNITURE.

For all Field and Mounted Officers, the same as for Officers of the Field Batteries.

NOTES.

The Sword-Belt—to be fitted so that the rear ring will appear between the hip buttons, and the front ring immediately over the left hip; and is never to be worn without the sword.

Straps—to be worn to the trousers on all occasions, except when in marching order on foot.

Pouch-Belt—to be worn at all times when on duty.

REGULATION FOR DRESS OF THE OFFICERS OF THE FIELD TRAIN DEPARTMENT.

For CHIEF COMMISSARY ranking as { LIEUTENANT-COLONEL.
„ COMMISSARY - ditto - MAJOR.
„ ASSISTANT-COMMISSARY ditto - CAPTAIN.
„ DEPUTY ASSISTANT-COMMISSARY } ditto - SUBALTERN.

DRESS.

Coat—blue tunic; single-breasted, with red stand-up collar and cuff; the collar without lace, the sleeve trimmed according to corresponding grade in the Artillery.

Buttons—Artillery.

Hat—cocked, plain, with gold loop and tassels.

Trousers—blue cloth, with a stripe of gold lace, one inch and three-quarters wide, down the outer seam.

Swords and Scabbards—Artillery pattern; brass for Officers with Field rank, steel for other ranks.

Sword-Knot—gold cord, and acorn.

Sword-Belt—black leather, with slings, to be worn over the coat.

Stock—black silk.

Gloves—white leather.

Shell-Jacket—Artillery pattern, but without "grenadier" on the collar, to be worn only in tropical climates.

UNDRESS.

Frock-Coat—dark blue cloth; the rank to be shown on the sleeve, in like manner as on the coat, but in black cord and lace.

Trousers—blue cloth, with scarlet stripe one inch and three quarters wide down the outer seam.

Forage-Cap—to be of dark blue cloth, with patent leather straight peak; band of gold one inch and seven tenths wide.

Cloak—blue, lined with white.

Spurs—Artillery pattern.

BARRACK-MASTERS.

DRESS.

The same in every respect as that prescribed for Military Storekeepers, vide page 152, with the exception of the sword-belt plate and button, of which patterns are deposited at the War Office.

DISTINCTIONS OF RANK.

1st Class Barrack Masters, as Deputy Military Storekeepers.

2nd Class Barrack Masters, as Assistant Military Storekeepers.

MILITARY STOREKEEPERS.

Coat—Tunic, blue, single-breasted, with scarlet collar, cuffs and slash on sleeve. The collar rounded off in front, cuff round, two and three-quarter inches deep, and ten and a half round; slashed flap on sleeve six inches long and two and a quarter inches wide, with three loops of half-inch lace, staff pattern, and uniform buttons; eight buttons in front at equal distances. The skirt ten and a half inches deep for an officer 5 feet 9 inches in height, with a variation of half an inch, longer or shorter, for every inch of difference in the height of the wearer; blue flap on the skirt behind, ten inches deep, two buttons on flap, and one on waist, with three loops of half-inch lace. The coat, collar, cuffs, and flaps, edged with scarlet cloth, quarter-inch, and the skirts lined with scarlet.

Distinctions of rank according to the relative ranks in the army, viz.:—

 Principal Military Storekeepers and Military Storekeepers as Lieutenant-Colonels, the collar laced round the top and bottom with a crown at each end of the collar.

 Deputy Military Storekeeper as Major, the same lace with a star.

 Assistant Military Storekeeper as Captain, lace round the top only of the collar, a crown and star in silver, at each end.

1st class Clerks as Lieutenants, the same lace with a crown.
2d class Clerks as Ensigns, the same lace with a star.

The Officers ranking with Field Officers to have two rows of half-inch lace round the top of the cuff, an edging of the same on the sleeve and skirt flaps, and down the edge of the skirts behind.

The Officers under that rank to have one row of lace round the cuff, none on the skirts, and the loops only on the skirt and sleeve flaps.

Lace—gold, staff pattern, half-inch width.

Buttons—gilt, with the crown and " Military Store" raised thereon.

Hat—cocked, the fan or back part nine inches, the front seven inches and a half, each corner five inches, uniform buttons, gold lace loop, and tassels of good crape fringe, with crimson underneath.

Trousers—blue cloth, with a gold stripe, one and three-quarter inches wide, staff pattern, down the outward seam.

Boots—Wellington.

Sword—the same as for Officers of Infantry.

Scabbard—brass for Officers ranking as Field Officers, steel for all other ranks.

Sword Knot—crimson and gold, with acorn tassel.

Sword-belt—plain black morocco, with slings and gilt hook, to be worn over the coat.

Plate—a round gilt clasp with V.R., surmounted by a crown in silver upon the centre-piece, and " Military Store" with a laurel branch also in silver on the outer circle.

Stock—black silk.

Gloves—white leather.

Forage-Cap—blue cloth with black leather peak and chin strap, scarlet band with " V.R.," surrounded by a wreath surmounted by a crown embroidered in gold on the front, with black button and trimming on the top.

Cloak—blue, lined with scarlet, of pattern for Officers of Infantry, with uniform buttons.

L

EQUERRIES TO THE QUEEN.

The dress and appointments of the Queen's Equerries are the same as those of Her Majesty's Aides-de-Camp, with the exception that the scarlet dress and undress coats have four buttons and loops upon the sleeve-flaps, instead of three.

Equerries holding the rank of General Officer wear cocked hat, plume, sash, button, sword and sword-belt of their rank.

In undress the Equerries are permitted to wear their regimental, or other uniform, with the aiguillette. With the blue undress coat, which is the same as that ordered for the Queen's A.D.C., plain Oxford grey trousers are to be worn without stripe.

Forage-Cap—the same as that for the Queen's A.D.C.
Great-Coat—same as for Queen's A.D.C.
Horse-Furniture—same as for Queen's A.D.C.

EQUERRIES OF THE ROYAL FAMILY.

Coat—scarlet single-breasted tunic, with eight holes and buttons in fore part; blue collar and cuffs, the collar rounded in front, with one embroidered frog loop; scarlet sleeve-flap, with four embroidered frog loops and buttons. Skirt fourteen inches long, lined with white; scarlet flaps on the skirts behind ten inches long, with three embroidered frog loops; two buttons at the waist and three on each flap. The front, hind-skirt, flaps, and top of collar edged with white, quarter inch.

Embroidery—gold; upon the collar, cuffs, and skirts, to be of the same pattern as worn by Her Majesty's Equerries.

Button—gilt, with a crown and military edge, of size and form prescribed for Infantry.

Aiguillette—gold, on the right shoulder, two-thirds of the size of the aiguillette of the Queen's Equerries; a cord on the left shoulder to match the sash.

Trousers—blue, with gold lace, same as for A.D.C.

Sash—of the officer's rank or regiment, worn over the left shoulder.

Sword-Belt—Russia leather embroidered belt and plate of the staff pattern for A.D.C. to General Officer.

Sword—of the staff pattern.

Sword-Knot—ditto.

Cocked-Hat and *Great-Coat* } the same as Her Majesty's Equerries.

www.ingramcontent.com/pod-product-compliance
Lightning Source LLC
Chambersburg PA
CBHW032123090426
42743CB00007B/442